The
Field Sales Manager's
Problem Solver

The Field Sales Manager's Problem Solver

Paul Micali

HAWTHORN BOOKS, INC.
Publishers/NEW YORK
A Howard & Wyndham Company

To all the ambitious people who have
selected sales and sales management as a
career—my daughter Donna included.

Contents

Introduction

Thousands of theories, formulas, and rules have been written to guide sales managers into the world of success. The dos and don'ts have been clearly spelled out and the theories scientifically backed by statistical research. On paper it all looks so good, so practical. It makes sense.

However, let's realize once and for all that the many variables interjected by human behavior change the picture substantially—sometimes beyond recognition. The ironclad theories, most of them developed by college professors who have never lived through it, go down the drain on a daily basis. The struggling field sales manager, constantly faced with a myriad of problems (and the more salespeople there are to supervise, the more problems there are) repeatedly wonders why the theories don't always work.

After twenty-five years of sales management experience, I don't claim to know all of the answers. No one ever will. But I have lived through enough experiences to have learned, at times the hard way, that the realistic solutions to many problems in this profession rarely follow theory. In fact, in many instances, the best approach to the sales manager's job is shockingly opposed to what's considered normal and routine.

That's what this book is all about. It touches upon the many problems encountered by a field sales manager and brings out the possible solutions from an experience and real-life standpoint. Some of the techniques or tactics used to produce the proper end result may surprise you. They may even shock you. But you must keep an open mind. Success rarely comes easily; all of us know that. However, it can be achieved more quickly if the seeker remains adaptable.

Speaking of success, are you aware that the average sales manager in the United States holds a job only four years? A frightening statistic, to say the least. But every four years, on the average, a company will change its sales manager. (This is true of district managers, regional managers, zone managers, etc.) Of course, some of these changes are caused by promotions. But the majority are for the opposite reason. Many top management officials blame it on the Peter Principle. Others claim that many sales managers burn themselves out. Then there is the old saying that as you climb higher on the ladder of success, the rungs get more slippery. There are a host of speculative reasons. And then there's the real reason: Sales managers simply foul themselves up. What does that mean? Just this: In the eyes of top management, the sales manager made one mistake too many. A mistake in judgment regarding sales personnel usually gets top billing. After all, each mistake made by a salesperson out in the field reflects upon the sales manager to whom that person reports. "Why was that individual hired?" they ask, or, "Why wasn't there closer supervision?"

But don't worry about this four-year thing. Worry solves nothing. That statistic doesn't have to affect *you*. Not as long as you do what you're doing right now—trying to find out how you can do your job better. I'm sure that your company has outlined your duties and responsibilities for you. Yet it's a sure bet that the company has *not* given you a compilation of all the mistakes made by your various predecessors or the theories that didn't work or the deviations from company policy that had to be instituted. Why? Because such a compilation usually just doesn't exist.

So what are the alternatives? Maybe many. One, however, should be obvious. You train yourself, constantly, to improve your skills, and reading this book is a step in the right direction.

1
General Problems of a Field Sales Manager

Since you were appointed field sales manager, district manager, or whatever your present title may be, you have been extremely busy. You have been completely involved in any number of field activities, from putting out fires in one territory or another to handling personnel problems, and you have begun to wonder exactly what your responsibilities are.

Are Your Job Responsibilities Clear?

Most companies do not specifically pinpoint the responsibilities of a field sales manager. In fact, the amount of freedom and creativity allowed by the home office is usually generous. In some cases, it's almost as though the powers that be say to the newly appointed field sales manager, "Here is a district. You may have *x* number of salespeople. Now go out and do the job." This might sound overly simplified, but talk to some seasoned field sales managers and they'll be quick to agree that this is about what it amounts to when you look back at the direction you've been given. Those who are creative thinkers, who are not afraid to try something new, who are willing to take full charge and responsibility for their actions, and who are willing to work hard to make success come about, don't worry that much about what their responsibilities really are. But, like other jobs where repetitiveness of activities is prevalent, it is a good idea every so often to review one's real responsibilities and make certain that the ship is on course.

The first corrective measure, obviously, is to look to one's position description. I realize that, to this day, there are still many companies which do not have an up-to-date position description for their field managers. That's really a crime. As products become more sophisticated, and as economic conditions change, the need for updating a field manager's position description becomes extremely important. So that's the first step. Make out your position description and go over it carefully with your superiors. Make certain that it is as up-to-date as possible and that your responsibilities are clearly defined. At least that will give you a good track on which your activities should run.

But whatever your position description dictates, you can rest assured that your responsibilities are not that unclear. They may be cluttered with all sorts of details, but the real, honest-to-goodness responsibilities of a field sales manager are completely obvious. They may easily be categorized into two main functions:

- Take the necessary action to keep all territories filled.
- Bring about, through your sales force, as many sales as are possible within your assigned area.

Each of these functions, naturally, is closely related to the other. In order for you to hire new sales representatives for new or unproductive territories from a budgetarily sound basis, you must have the other territories in a healthy condition. That is, they must be producing substantial sales to warrant this additional overhead on your part. On the other hand, you cannot bring in all of the possible sales in a given area unless coverage is as complete as a full complement of salespeople would make it. So both functions are extremely important and require equal attention.

And let's get something straight right now. There is a worn-out rationalization made by sales managers that goes like this: "I'd rather leave a territory open and be satisfied with the existing business that comes in rather than hire a mediocre sales representative just to have it covered." That's exactly what it is—a rationalization, and a bad one at that. Open territories may produce *some* sales through advertising efforts by the company or through spillover (the residual effect from the previous sales representative). But the sales curve of an open territory always heads downward. It doesn't take very long for the curve to flatten out at a very low level. The sales manager who mouths such a rationalization is the very same individual who either finds the recruiting aspects of the job boring or who is a slow self-motivator and often fails to get a job done quickly.

There are many activities that you will engage in from time to time in the process of discharging your duties as a sales manager. But don't ever be confused over what your primary functions are.

What Takes Priority?

Every time the phone rings or the mail arrives, you are faced with new problems, new details that must be attended to. At times they will bunch up to such a degree that you wonder how you will find the time to do everything that needs to be done. In addition to time, however, there is still another problem that compounds the situation. What should be done first? You ask yourself this almost regularly, wondering where the priorities really lie.

There is that human tendency, you know, to do just those things we like to do best. This is not always a good solution to the problem because what we might like to do might not be the thing that should be done on a priority basis.

In order to solve the problem of priorities for yourself, it is important to understand the real meaning behind your title. "Manager," that's what you are. What do you manage? You manage sales representatives. What does that mean? It means that everyone reporting to you looks to you for leadership and proper supervision (guidance). The home office looks to you for leadership in your area and proper supervision of your people. It's not that hard to see. There are a group of individuals whose responsibility it is to make sales calls and bring in sales for the company. It is your responsibility to make sure that the job is done right. You can only do this through leadership, supervision—better known as guidance in sales work—and, of course, the proficiency necessary to properly motivate everyone in your employ. Now, let's note how this is applied. Let's take three of the many situations that may well come up in the course of a day:

1. The home office wants more input for next year's budget.
2. A note from an applicant states that she needs answers to two questions before accepting your job offer.
3. One of your salesmen has written you that his expense check is two weeks overdue.

In what order would you handle these situations? Test yourself. Read no further.

The logical order for attention to these situations is 3, 2, 1. The reasons, upon reflection, make sense. Your first responsibility is to your salesman who is running out of expense money. You are a leader. He looks to you for leadership. So you handle that one first. Then, we already said how important it is to maintain a full complement of sales representatives by filling all territories as quickly as possible. If an individual needs answers to two questions and is ready to accept your job offer, this requires quick action. The sooner the job is accepted, the sooner your territory is filled. Now, I don't mean to imply that the home office gets last billing. In some instances it, too, requires immediate attention. But in this case, they are asking for information regarding *next year's* budget. You certainly wouldn't sacrifice your own salesman or an applicant who is ready to join you for something that is being planned for *next year*.

All right, you say, such alignment of priorities does make sense, but what are you supposed to do? Look over everything that has come up and decide which is to be done first? Exactly. Only when you give priority to the deserving situations can you call yourself a real manager. Besides, there is another theory involved. By doing the most important thing first, each day, you will know that the most important thing got done. That may sound trite, but how many times have you found yourself handling all sorts of trivial matters only to discover that time has run out and a much more important task has to be put off until tomorrow or next week.

Really, when it's all said and done, it's a case of organization. If you get yourself into the habit of organizing what you're going to do each day, you will automatically avoid problems of priority. Here's how it works. Always carry a small notebook on your person, preferably one with a date on each page covering the month. Then, each day, depending on what has transpired in the early morning, such as mail, phone calls, and carry-overs from the previous day, you list the matters that you will attend to in order of priority. As you take care of each item, you cross it off. At the end of the day the items that you did not get to, and these are known as carry-overs, will be transferred to the next day's agenda—but not until the next day begins. You see, something else may come up tomorrow morning that will take precedence over the less important items that didn't get done today.

Where Do Obligations Lie?

You have been frustrated on many occasions. It can be worse than being torn between two lovers. You find yourself having to cope with four groups of people. Yes, four different groups of people. Specifically, they represent your sales force, your management officials, your associates, and all of the customers in your area of responsibility. You're not entirely certain just how much you owe to whom and when you should drop your attention from one group to give it to another.

This can be a substantial problem, especially for the new field sales manager. After all, all four of these groups are important. Attention to detail is important no matter which group demands it. Sometimes people who simply ask should be doing the demanding and vice versa. And the problem is right on your lap. You have to decide which way to turn.

Your first and foremost obligation is to your sales force. As we said, they look to you for leadership. They depend upon you for many things. Your personal success is ultimately measured by what you get done *through* them. So obviously, when you decide that your most important obligation is to them, you are also insuring and securing your own future. And your company will never fault you for this because the purpose of assigning you the task of being a field sales manager was to get the most out of the people who would report to you. So never refrain from putting yourself out for any one member of your sales staff. If it takes you away from something else that you'd rather be doing, if it takes an evening of your time that you would have rather spent enjoying yourself at the movies, or if a situation cuts into your weekend, remember that your obligation lies with the sales force. You are doing what you are supposed to be doing most of the time.

You have no idea how many sales representatives will cry the blues when they think that they are neglected by their sales manager. It can almost sound childish. I have heard grown men say to me, "I know you've been awfully busy hiring new men, but you haven't worked with me for three months. You haven't forgotten me, have you?" Mind you, I probably had been in touch with the individual on a weekly basis either through memoranda or phone calls. Salespeople who spend a tremendous amount of time alone in their cars, going from sales call to sales call, have time to think. Since they don't see a superior on a daily basis, they tend to feel neglected if contact is lacking. With some, morale is affected. With others it could even precipitate an "I don't care" attitude. Meaning, "If my manager doesn't care about me, then I don't care about my job. So why make more sales calls than are absolutely necessary to keep my job?"

It follows, therefore, that regular contact with your sales staff is a must. On that score, you have a definite, ongoing obligation. And while relationships between you and your people will vary from person to person, one aspect will remain constant. They will always know that you are constantly concerned about them and this is a fine quality of leadership. Here is a good rule of thumb in this regard: Never let more than a week go by without having some contact with each member of your sales staff. This does not have to be personal contact. It can just as well be a phone call or even a written memorandum. But the point is, you are in touch. Furthermore, you cannot expect your people regularly to submit reports on time if they never hear from you. It's a two-way street. If they owe you a report of some sort and they hear from you, they are automatically reminded of that report and feel an inner obligation to get it to you, even though you haven't even mentioned it.

The name of the game may be leadership, but with leadership comes responsibilities and obligations. Your first and foremost obligation is to your sales force.

Right behind your sales force comes management. Yes, to management you certainly have a strong obligation as well. Your superiors entrusted in you a very important responsibility when they placed you out in the field, on your own and in charge of a group of salespeople. Obviously, they have a lot of faith in you. But I can assure you that that faith can be shaken, particularly when results are not forthcoming. But that isn't the only concern of management. In addition to results, they like to know what's going on. If there is anything that disturbs management officials, it's when they learn something from a particular area of the country and have to track down the field sales manager to get the details. They would much prefer to have obtained the information as quickly as possible directly from the field sales manager. Management always looks upon a field sales manager as an extension of the home office management. They expect him to be in close communication with home office officials, much the same as he would be if he were headquartered at the home office. It is extremely rare when a field sales manager is told to reduce his number of phone calls to the home office or to cut down on the postage he is using when writing in. This is practically unheard of. The more contact, the better. This is not to be construed that the contact becomes a way of obtaining permission for every move made. Far from it. That kind of contact would lose a field sales manager many brownie points. You are expected to make your own decisions and to sink or swim with them. But to inform management officials of whatever decisions you have made is considered good judgment on your part. At least they know what you are doing and when. I might add, at this juncture, that contact with management officials has much political value—a fact that cannot be dismissed too lightly. Whenever you write to your superior at the home office, you can be sure that several people will see that piece of correspondence. Certainly a secretary will. Perhaps, in the absence of your superior, another member of management of equal stature may be given the correspondence for whatever action it might require. Then, there will be times when you will send in certain information that may have marketing significance or is considered vital to the manufacturing area or to the market research department or to any other segment of the company. In such cases you may rest assured that your correspondence will be photocopied in order that appropriate individuals may be informed of its contents. Under such circumstances your name and your activities are attracting specific attention. It doesn't hurt.

But, above all this, management expects proper representation by a field sales manager. The company policies are to be upheld. The loyalty of all salespeople must be to the company, and only the field sales manager can make certain of that. Management expects much from a sales manager but is willing to give equally as much when asked. Good rapport is essential. In the process of maintaining that rapport the astute field sales manager makes absolutely certain that management is kept informed on all counts. That is an obligation that may not be clearly spelled out but nevertheless must be faced.

What about your obligation to associates such as product managers, neighboring field sales managers, market researchers, product development specialists, and all the other staff individuals who depend upon line managers like yourself for bits and pieces of information that help them solve their own puzzles? It is absolutely ridiculous to develop the attitude that all of the people outside of the sales function are unimportant. And believe me, in many companies such an attitude does exist. The sales department assumes the attitude that its members bring in the bacon. Without them the company could never survive. So, "We're the most important and we don't have to bother with anyone else." Such an attitude is a sad mistake. Every player on a baseball team is important. The same is true in business. Every department in the company is important. It's teamwork all the way. Salespeople must never forget that the promotion behind their sales efforts makes them look good, the research and development gives them products to sell in future years, and almost every other department of the company backs them up on a regular basis.

A good manager never forgets all this and makes certain that all lines of communication are always open with any and all other people in the company who are interested in what's going on in sales generally and in his own area specifically. In fact, your obligation doesn't really end there. It's a good idea, whenever you're in the home office, to visit with as many of these people as possible. It doesn't take long to stop in and say hello. In the process, your relationships are strengthened and communication is encouraged. What seems, many times, as insignificant information in the field, becomes extremely important to certain individuals in the home office. Many of them live in what might be termed a cocoon. They are only aware of what goes on in the field when they are told by you or the other field managers. Otherwise, they have no alternative but to make assumptions—and that can be dangerous. In almost every company there is the concentrated effort, from time to time, to get staff people out in the field to find out what is really going on. Somehow, however, it never comes about to any great degree. Staffers get so involved with home office activities that there is rarely time to make a swing through a particular area for informational purposes.

So it all boils down to how much you are willing to cooperate. It is very easy, more often than not, to forget this obligation to associates or to take it very lightly.

Here's an example. Home office staffers are always hungry for competitive information. They want to know what competition is doing in the way of product promotion, pricing, deals, returns, back-ordering—just about anything the competition is doing. But how are they going to find out? It's difficult to write or phone large customers, who may resent it or may even refuse to answer any questions. Their best source is the sales force. Their own sales force. And you are in charge of a segment of that sales force. So they look to you and your people for this information. What happens? Many times a salesperson will run across competitive information by simply overhearing a conversation. She may learn of a price drop by a competitor. However, she decides that since she's not covering a territory in a large metropolitan area, what she heard was not information that's as new as it sounds. Besides, she assumes, the home office probably knows all about it. How unfortunate. If everyone were to assume that the home office must know about it, the home office may never learn about it. It is also quite possible that the price cut is being tested in a particular area of the country to see if it increases sales of a particular product. This could be vital information to your home office. They may very well be doing the very same thing in another part of the country or may be contemplating such a maneuver. This is only one of many similar obligations, and your job is to keep your associates in mind at all times and to make sure that your sales staff recognizes their importance by following through for you.

Don't forget the customers. Yes, the field sales manager does have an obligation to the customers. They like your attention. Particularly the large customers. To them it is fundamental that the sales rep's superior should stop in every so often and pay some attention to an account of their size. But it goes further than that. Customers are people; they have egos and they like to feel that the company appreciates their business. And while the sales rep might transmit such a feeling, they are still flattered when someone in a supervisory capacity comes in to see them. They enjoy such contact with the "upper echelon." It makes them feel important. And, in return, they will many times give you information that your salespeople would never get.

Certainly it is not difficult to give customers the attention they deserve. While working with your sales representatives out in the field you make sales calls with them. Each call represents a marvelous opportunity to get to know the customer. I am not suggesting that you usurp time from the sales call itself. First the salesman should make his usual presentation, ask for the order, etc. But before leaving, it's a good idea for you to have a chat with the customer. Cement relations by getting to know the account better. Be careful, though, that you don't fall into the usual pattern of answering such questions as "How much area do you cover?" or "How many salespeople do you have?" It is much better if you control the conversation so that you are asking the customer questions. The more he talks about himself, the more flattered he will be. And the happier he will feel that he has had contact with you. Besides, while talking about himself and his business he may very well give you information that could prove valuable.

So, when it's all said and done, you will have many-faceted obligations to your sales force, to management, to your associates within the company, and to your customers. As we have discussed, there are definite priorities in meeting these obligations. But the problem is not so much the priorities involved, but the realization of the obligations themselves. The picture is substantially clear.

2
Supervision of Salespeople

Bill Graham's sales productivity has definitely reached a plateau. This has now been the case for six months. You have been asking him to develop some accounts in the west part of Haytown. You know that there's business there. But he doesn't do it. Every time you bring up the subject, he claims that the area and the people in it give him the creeps. He passes it off laughingly each time—and changes the subject on you. You had planned to put your foot down at each of these occasions, but you didn't. Why?

Just because you couldn't, that's why. You couldn't because Bill is not just one of your salesmen, he's also a close friend. Fairly often you go fishing with him and you also play golf together. Every two or three weeks you get together with your wives on a Saturday for dinner and a night on the town. Your wife is on the same bowling team with Bill's. In fact, the relationship is so close that when Shirley Graham had to be rushed to the hospital to deliver their second child at 3:00 A.M. one morning, Bill phoned you, and you gladly rushed over to baby-sit with their little boy.

Under such circumstances, how could you possibly get tough with Bill when he doesn't respect your wishes? The problem is that he doesn't respect you as his superior. He respects you as a close friend, most definitely. But not as a boss. It's a big problem in supervision. One that you have usually created all by yourself.

Are Your Employees Your Buddies?

There are many theories on how much familiarity you can allow to develop and most of them are riddled with temperance, variables, and rationalizations. Take it from one who has been over this road enough times to know. There are definite, clear-cut rules to be followed. For openers: *Always stay at arm's length from your salespeople*. This does not mean that you play the part of a mean, unfriendly militarist. Not at all. It's okay to be friendly, pleasant, and understanding. In fact, it's necessary. That's the only way to promote a spirit of cooperation, a willingness to communicate and a high level of good morale. But you always draw that fine line that must exist between you and your salespeople. And you must never cross it.

While it's desirable to have a sales rep call you by your first name, it does not follow that this "friendship" prevents you from issuing an order. There's a big difference between issuing a direct order and pussyfooting an issue because of friendly relationships. When Bill hears your friendly voice saying, "I do hope you'll get to West Haytown one of these days," he can joke about it and forget it. But had you said, "Bill, I *want* you to spend next week at West Haytown and I'll be eager to see how many accounts you open," the reaction would have been quite different. You see, when the existing relationship has been properly conditioned, you can say things like, "I want," "I expect," "You must," "Do it my way," etc. And such orders will be followed. They won't be shrugged off with, "Well, Jack's a good guy, and I'll talk my way out of it."

Simply remember that, as a field sales manager, you are the main contact your salespeople have with your company's management officials. You *are* the company. So not only is the dignity of the company at stake, but so is your ability to direct the sales operations of those who report to you. And that ability is preserved by following some time-tested guidelines:

- Don't engage in sporting activities regularly with members of your staff.
- Don't socialize with them routinely.
- Do visit their homes, but only in the case of a serious illness, a death, a tragedy—instances in which your absence would be most noticeable.
- Don't accept invitations to parties at their homes. Not all of them will have parties, and those that do may use them to cement a relationship with you.
- Don't invite certain members of your staff to your home. It displays favoritism. Invite them all—for a party—*once a year* (perhaps at Christmastime). That's often enough.
- Don't condone the development of close relationships between your spouse and the spouses of your salespeople.
- Don't encourage regular contact, especially through sports, between your children and theirs.

- Don't suggest that a new employee about to relocate, buy the available house on your street (and thereby become your neighbor as well).
- Don't volunteer to sponsor any of your people for membership at your golf club, yacht club, tennis club, etc.

Are You Being Lied To?

How disappointed you were the day you found out that Carl King had told you an outright lie. You had asked him to stop in and see an irate customer in Littleton about a product complaint. After you knew that he had made a swing through Littleton, you asked Carl if he had stopped in. He said yes and explained how he handled Mrs. Sampson. He assured you that everything was now okay. Then, two days later, Sampson called you and screamed that no one had yet bothered to stop in to see her. You meekly said that you thought that King had been there, and this added fuel to the fire. "No one, absolutely no one, *I said*, has been here," she bellowed.

Why does this happen? And it happens more than you would expect. Much more than any sales manager likes.

There are a variety of reasons behind the lying problem, and each has a specific solution. Here are a few of them:

1. *Some people lie habitually.* They regularly tell a little white lie, here and there, to get out of a tight situation. This doesn't bother them, particularly when they've only twisted the truth somewhat. It's been said that salespeople do to the truth what whipping does to cream—they change the consistency a little bit. But a continuance of this habit only gets them in deeper. Soon they tell bigger lies without batting an eyelash. And before long they are telling

volved begin to realize that if they keep you regularly disappointed in them, they can never afford a dip in sales. The latter, combined with a poor image, could spell doom—known as replacement. This realization usually brings about corrective action.

You have probably encountered a number of other reasons why your people have lied to you. If not, you will. It is definitely a problem and one that must be met head on. The biggest mistake would be to let a lie slip by unnoticed purposely. You may do so as you rationalize that it's not important enough to make an issue of it. But let someone who lies get away with it and you are promoting bigger and better lies.

I have had many experiences that proved this point too well. One of them was a classic. For months I had been looking for someone to fill the tri-city territory of Albany–Schenectady–Troy, New York. It seemed that qualified pharmaceutical sales applicants in that area just didn't exist. So, while interviewing in Boston for my bullpen one day, I came across a bright young man who was most impressive. He wanted very much to join our company. So I tested this strong desire by asking, "Would you be willing to move to an open territory I happen to have?" He jumped at it. No problem. But I wanted to make sure. So, later that week, I had lunch with him and his wife. I asked *her* if moving to upstate New York from Worcester, Massachusetts, would bother her in any way. She said, "Not at all. Our son is only three years old, and schooling is not a problem." When I reminded her that her roots, all her relatives, and his as well, were in Worcester, she said that she belonged wherever her husband happened to be to further his career. I was convinced, offered Jim the territory, and he quickly accepted.

I sent the paperwork to the home office, and as soon as the personnel department completed a more intensive check on his background, they informed me that he had been dismissed from a state summer job for having lied about his age. I pondered over this but rationalized that since it happened while he was still young and in school, I could easily chalk it up to immaturity. I'm sure now that my anxiety to fill the territory played an important part in my rationalization. I also decided to forgo mentioning this to Jim—a big mistake.

How pleased I was at the rapidity with which Jim moved his family to Troy, New York, and started work. Once a month I worked with him on territory. He made steady progress. His sales figures were not remarkable, but he produced a respectable increase each month. At the end of the first day of each two-day field visit, I would have dinner with Jim and would ask him to bring along his wife. Each time, however, there was some reason why she couldn't make it.

One day the company announced a price reduction on a very competitive product. A telegram from the home office instructed me to phone all sales representatives who, in turn, would phone all major accounts. That evening I reached everyone but Jim. There was no answer at his home. And early the next morning and throughout the day and evening there was no answer, either. I knew that they lived in a two-family house owned by the people who occupied the first floor. So, I convinced the telephone operator to give me the landlord's number, and I phoned. Mrs. Shaw answered.

"Terribly sorry to bother you, Mrs. Shaw, but it is very important that I reach my salesman, Jim Wilcox.

He hasn't answered his phone in two days, and I'm worried that there might be something wrong.''

"Well, there certainly is, you might say. They haven't lived upstairs for months. They pay the rent, and I can't complain, but it just doesn't seem right."

"That's most surprising, isn't it? Mrs. Shaw, did they actually move the furniture out?"

"Oh, yes. About a month after they moved in, she left with the baby. He lived there alone for about two weeks after that. Then the moving van came, and all the furniture was taken out. I saw Mr. Wilcox that day, and he said that they were getting new furniture, which wouldn't be delivered for a while. I could tell from the expression on his face that he wasn't telling the truth. Since the place has been empty, we've been getting the rent check by mail every month—and no return address on the envelope. If you find him, please tell him that we would rather rent to some-one else. It's not fair for us to take money for nothing, and we'll forget about the lease. Too bad. They seemed like such nice young folks.''

A lovely lady, who really opened up. But now I knew I had a real problem. I looked at my copy of Jim's itinerary. He was scheduled to call on his largest wholesale account the next day. Chances were that he would. It's where he got his biggest order each month. So, early the following morning I called the wholesaler and left word for Jim to call me when he came in. When I heard from him, late morning, I told him that there was something important that I needed to discuss with him. I asked him to meet me at the Albany airport at 4:30 that afternoon. He was waiting when my plane landed. He greeted me with his usual jovial smile.

In the coffee shop the conversation went like this:

"Jim, I tried to reach you regarding a price reduction, and no one answered your phone day or night."

"Well, Mary's mother has been ill in Worcester, and she went over for a few days. I've been staying with a friend while she's away."

"How long has Mary been away?"

"Only a few days."

"You mean that if I had called you last week, I would have reached you?"

"Oh, sure."

"Jim, your family, as well as your furniture, have been out of your apartment for the last five months. I talked with Mrs. Shaw, your landlady, last night. Now, come clean. What's the story?"

His face turned beet red. It took him a minute or two to regain his composure. Then he began to explain:

"We were here two weeks and Mary said that she was too lonesome. I told her that we would soon make new friends, but that didn't seem to matter. How could we, anyway—we spent every weekend in Worcester at her mother's. So, after we had been here five weeks, she went back for good. What choice did I have? She found a place, and we moved the furniture. Believe me, it hasn't been easy, what with paying two rents and commuting."

"Commuting? This territory is at least 125 miles from Worcester, with no major highway."

"I know, I leave the house at 5:30 every morning."

"And when do you get home?"

"At 8:30 or 9:00 at night."

"This has been your schedule *every day*, Jim?"

"Well, most every day. Some mornings I've overslept, and some afternoons I've quit early."

I could feel for this man who was torn between his job and his family. Yet, all I could think of was how many sales calls weren't made over the last five months and how much better the territory could have done with proper coverage.

"Jim, how I wish you could have leveled with me when this first happened. At about the time that your wife went back to mother, I had an unexpected opening in the Boston area—because of a promotion—and I quickly filled it. That was 36 miles from Worcester, not 125. We could have worked something out. And many times I asked you how Mary liked the area. Each time you lied to me, saying she had 'totally adjusted.' "

I had already decided, before meeting Jim in Albany that I would terminate him. I just couldn't tolerate such deviousness. Yet when I heard his story, I had second thoughts. But only for a moment or two. Then I had to straighten myself out. I certainly couldn't live with the haphazard coverage that his commuting produced, nor did I have a territory in the area in which Mary's mother lived. And even if I did, how would I ever again know when Jim was telling me the truth?

Certain management decisions are hard to make, and many of them leave you feeling heartless. But they must be made. It wasn't easy to tell Jim that he was through, nor to meet him two days later to take his samples, literature, and company car. But I had no choice. In the supervision of salespeople, you must demand and obtain the truth about everything. Without it you just don't have a team with which you can win.

Is Your Control Slipping?

Last week you received two phone calls from two of your people. Joe told you that he was really in a fix in one of his accounts. He'd found some outdated merchandise (well over a year old) that he knew was not returnable. But since the manager of the store had given him a large order, he just couldn't refuse to take back the merchandise.

The other phone call was one in which Mary reported that she was able to obtain a large order but had to give a quantity price beyond the 12 percent limit. She allowed a 14 percent discount because of the size of the order and she claimed that there was no way she could have obtained the order without that discount.

In both cases you didn't like what you heard, but you quickly remembered the well-known theory that, as a member of sales management, you "always back up your salespeople." So, to both of them, you said something like, "Well, you shouldn't have done that, because it's against company policy, but since you did it, I'll back you up with the home office."

Now, what exactly is happening here? It's very obvious if you think about it. Your control is slipping. From here on in, with these two salespeople (and with any other members of your staff who do likewise) the amount of control that you will have will be negligible. Once they know that they will be backed up by you, no matter what the circumstances are, they will proceed to make judgments on territory without checking with you.

Of course, you can argue that you want the business. You don't want to lose those orders. Furthermore, you don't want to embarrass your salespeople, nor do you want to ruffle the feathers of those two customers. So you rationalize that really, you had no other choice but to do what you did.

Wrong! When you let things like this slip by, not only is your control slipping, but so is your image with the home office and possibly your forward progress in the company.

Two specific things have happened here:

- You allowed a major decision, against company policy, to be made by a salesperson on territory without your permission. That person could have asked for more time to obtain your permission if such was to be had.
- You were disloyal to the company. That's right, disloyal. One of your responsibilities as a field sales manager is to uphold company policies in the field. When you allow two of your people to break those policies and you approve such decisions, is this fair to the rest of your people, to the rest of the salespeople in the entire company, to the company itself?

We have already said that out in the field you *are* the company. You represent the home office and its policies. And since there are always sound reasons behind company policies, how seriously are you taking your management responsibilities when you allow them to be violated?

The answer to this problem is very clear-cut. Upon hiring a sales representative or upon taking over a district or a division, you make it quite clear that you are in charge. I realize that it is always a lot easier to do so when hiring an individual. At that point, the new hiree sees you as a very authoritative individual. After all, you're doing the hiring. You must be the boss. But it's a lot harder when you are facing an entire group, say, at a sales meeting, and you have to get across to them that you are in charge. It smacks of egotism, you say. And it doesn't promote a good relationship between sales manager and sales representative. It's hard to find the right words to use in order to come across in the proper fashion.

Well, one way to do it is simply to restate your responsibilities to the company. You tell them that you are in the field to uphold company policies and to make certain that they are not violated. Therefore, in order for you to discharge your own responsibilities, it becomes extremely important that your people look to you for direction and, even more crucial, do not make important decisions involving company policies without first obtaining your permission. Now, that's not so hard to understand, nor is it so hard to put into plain English.

But even if you can't word it as smoothly as you'd like, there is nothing wrong with the direct approach. A few years back I made a motivational film with Red Auerbach, president of the Boston Celtics. The whole world knows of the basketball dynasty built by Red over the years that he coached the Boston Celtics. Before becoming president and general manager, he had coached over a thousand NBA games and had won more world championships than any other team. In that film I asked Red to make a comparison between how he handled his players and how a sales manager should handle sales representatives. When we touched upon the subject of control, he said the following:

At the beginning of every season I gave my players the same talk. I would say to them, 'Let's understand one thing . . . I am the boss. There is no question that I am the boss because I can hire and fire anybody. I also control how much you earn. So I am the boss. Now, there are twelve of you and only one of me. Therefore, it makes sense that it is a lot easier for each of you to get to know what makes me tick than it would be for me to get to know what makes each one of you tick. So I expect each of you to know what makes me do what I do and why I do it. If you have any questions, ask. But that's the way it's going to be, and that's how we're going to have a winning team!'

As far as I'm concerned, sales managers should do the same thing. They should make it quite clear from the very beginning. Without control, you don't win.

Getting back to Joe and Mary, this is what you should have done. You should have told each of them to go back to their respective customers and explain that their promises cannot be upheld by the company. Embarrassing? You bet it is. But it also carries impact. In addition to the embarrassment, they will probably lose the two orders, or part of them. Yet, one thing is certain. They will never again violate company policies without getting your permission first. And if that permission is not forthcoming, they will finally realize that company policies are there for a reason and they will not continue to bother you with requests to violate them.

Like so many other things in sales management, if your control is slipping, it's because you allow it to. Do something about it at the earliest possible stage and you will avoid problems in the future.

Are Territorial Facts Hidden?

Roland is a better-than-average salesman whose daily reports show that he makes more calls than even the better salespeople who report to you. In addition to this observation, you have also noticed that he is not completely at ease when you work with him on territory. You also wonder why, when you are making routine calls together, there is always a reason to skip around and bypass certain customers who are on the way.

On the whole he is a likable fellow, and every single customer has nothing but praise for him when you are making calls together. This is very heartwarming, of course, and you never fail to compliment him on this aspect of his operation.

But there very definitely could be a problem here, even though it may not be obvious. It is quite possible that Roland is hiding territorial facts from you. What kind of facts? He may be avoiding certain customers who always give him a hard time about deliveries, quality, company policies, etc. He may also be making certain that prospective customers, to whom he has never been able to sell, are never in your presence. Nor are the smaller customers on whom he rarely calls but who are regularly listed in his daily report.

The answer, while relatively obvious, is many times ignored by a sales manager. In an effort to maintain good relationships and to make a sales representative feel completely at ease during a field visit, this is what usually happens: The sales manager arrives for a field visit, joins the sales representative either at the airport or at another designated location, and usually opens with the following remarks: "Please don't let my field visit interrupt your operation in any way. I want you to cover your territory according to whatever plan you had for today and I'll just tag along and help you in whatever way that I can." Now, that's almost like getting a license to steal. Given that carte blanche, the sales representative now makes sure that you are not taken anywhere that problems might be brewing. You will only be exposed to those accounts where the customer-company relationship is excellent.

Now, of what value is a field visit of this nature? It may promote an even better relationship with your sales representative, but by having territorial facts hidden from you, the whole visit becomes a superficial exercise with false results. You will also find that the more experienced your people are, the more adept they become at maneuvering your activities during a field visit. They always have the right answers as to why we need not call on that particular account today or why calling on a prospective account as a twosome might upset the apple cart. They also drive through the center of town both to waste time and to show you how difficult it is to cover that area. And for lunch they take you to a crowded restaurant where the service is slow to further reduce the amount of afternoon calling time.

Some sales managers don't consider this a problem, really. They take the position that one should not be a suspecting individual. They feel that if something is wrong in a territory, it will eventually come up. Well, it may take much longer than you bargained for. It's not a case of being suspecting. It's a case of being a good supervisor. When you go on a field visit, you want to know what's going on in that territory. You want to have the ability to dig if need be. You have the authority to call on anyone at any time. After all, it's your area as well as the sales representative's. And there is nothing like the element of surprise. For instance, as you're driving by a particular account and it's obvious that you're not going to be stopping there, why not say something like, "I've never been in that account. Let's stop." When you're told that the buyer is not there on Tuesdays, you counter with, "That doesn't matter. Let's stop anyway." You will be amazed at what will develop at accounts where there was opposition to making a call.

There is another fallacy that compounds this problem. Many sales managers have the mistaken notion that they have no business calling on an account alone without the sales representative. It's sneaky, they feel. It's not fair. It just shouldn't be done. Some of your people will even resent calls you make by yourself when there are territorial facts that they want hidden. When everything is aboveboard, there is never any problem. Besides, there will be times when one of your salespeople is on vacation and an account needs some attention. Naturally, you will be taking care of this alone. There will be other times when you will want to do some field research for the home office without involving the sales representative. What's wrong with calling on some large as well as small accounts to get a feel for a particular problem or opinions needed by the home office? Let's not forget, you are the boss. You have a right to step into any territory under your supervision and call on any account at any time. Any of your people who don't understand this, or who don't want to understand it, deserve careful scrutiny during field visits.

I found that whenever I insisted on seeing an account that was deliberately neglected whenever I was making a field visit, a problem usually existed. I can recall discovering that an account, which continually showed up in daily reports, had never been called on; a customer who was buying samples from my salesman; an account where one of my people was working evenings, against company policy. I repeat, when everything is aboveboard, there is never any objection to your digging in.

To avoid problems, or to discover them before they reach monstrous proportions, develop an inquisitive mind and never feel that you are too suspecting. Above all, beware of salespeople who come up with reasons why your field visit should be postponed or who ask for more advance notice.

Are Written Reports Late?

Every time you think of Jack Emerson, your blood pressure goes up. He's a better-than-average salesman, a real workhorse who "pounds the pavement" rain or shine. Always gives you an honest day's work. But to get reports out of him is an uphill battle all the way—every month.

Every sales manager has a Jack Emerson or two—or three—or??? They are a specific breed of salespeople who readily offer an explanation for this frustrating habit. Each will say, "I love to sell, but I hate paperwork." For the most part they're telling the truth. They get a thrill out of every order they write. Their orders are always sent in promptly. But all other reports are always late. Some very late. And sometimes you practically have to beg for them.

What good is an itinerary for a given month when you receive it on the twentieth of that month? Or a competitive information report on a product introduced four months ago? Or a weekly call report covering three weeks ago? Or a monthly recap of calls and orders that's two months old?

Reports represent a great supervisory tool. They help you to know where your people are, where they're going, who they're seeing and when, their ratio of calls to orders, etc. This information is vital. Without it your supervisory power is always affected.

It has been said that the supervision of outside salespeople, at best, is lousy. And rightly so. After all, they don't punch in at 9:00 and punch out at 5:00. There's no one looking over their shoulder. There's no way of knowing how long the lunch hours really are or how many "detours" are taken for personal reasons. So look at it this way. When one of your people has a dry day (not a single sale), all that you and your company have—for the cost involved—is a piece of paper. Yes, a report that at least tells you with whom the time was spent. Under such circumstances, why shouldn't you get that costly piece of paper—on time?

The trouble is that most people in sales consider the submission of reports a distasteful chore, particularly since, in most cases, reports are to be filled out on the off hours; never at the expense of selling time. Those with a strong sense of responsibility and who can muster the necessary willpower will regularly come through with reports on time. But what do you do with those who are negligent in this area?

Well, under any circumstance, you must never lose your temper. To display such a personality flaw would reflect on your leadership qualities. So you act very calmly, on the first offense, as you impress upon the delinquent that reports are extremely important. You explain that you must have them on time to do your own job properly and you also add that punctuality with reports is a significant factor in the performance evaluation of sales representatives.

On the second offense you must take action of more official nature. This is best done by writing the individual a memorandum along the following lines:

To: Jack Emerson   Date:
From: Bill Manager
Subject: Late Reports

I have not received your monthly report of territorial activities, and it is late by two weeks. Last month, on October 19 specifically, when you submitted a late itinerary for that month, I impressed upon you that *all* reports *must* be submitted on time. The procedures are clearly defined in your sales manual and were thoroughly covered during your training.

I will expect to receive your activities report by return mail and trust that all of your future reports will be submitted on time—a requisite of your employment agreement.

cc: J. J. H, Mktg. V.P.
Personnel File

It must be noted that a memorandum of this type has dual impact. A slap on the wrist in writing usually causes the recipient to reread the message two or three times. This makes a deep impression. Second, when the individual sees where the two copies were directed, further impact is produced, and the seriousness of the situation is more fully realized. Surveys have shown that people respond to information received through the eyes 87 percent of the time and to that received through the ears only 7 percent of the time. This vast difference cannot be ignored.

On the *third* offense, especially if it comes on the heels of the second, drastic action is indicated. Just how drastic depends upon the person's sales record and general performance. If your evaluation of the individual in these categories is average or below, it's time for a full-fledged counseling session, at which time you pull no punches. You make it extremely clear that his or her sales record is not so commendable that liberties with company policies can be taken. Not that they are ever tolerated, but that under the circumstances they are dealt with even more sternly. In fact, you explain, "We have come to the point that unless reports are on time from now on, the result may well be termination of employment." The reaction you get to this approach will be most significant. If the attitude is of deep concern, bordering on shock over such drastic measures, chances are that you have corrected the problem. (That it had to be done through the instilling of fear is regrettable, but some people simply don't understand any other language.) On the other hand, if the attitude is of the opposite nature—relaxed, unconcerned, almost defiant—you have learned that it's time to do something about a replacement. Just bear in mind as you make the decision that your success as a sales manager requires that you follow certain specific time-tested ground rules. One of them is: *There is no room in an effective sales force for an average sales representative who is lax in submitting reports.*

On occasion you'll have a good sales producer who makes more calls than average, is heavily involved in community affairs, has an excellent attitude about everything, but is sometimes late with reports. Over the years I have used a variety of motivational techniques on people who fell in this particular category, some working better than others. But the one that seemed to work best was the easiest to administer: I simply held up the individual's expense check (not the salary check—that's illegal). I reasoned that for my people to be paid for expenses incurred I needed more proof than expense reports. I needed to know where the time was spent, with whom, when, how many calls were made, what sales resulted, etc. Then, and only then, were expenses justified. To me, reports constitute the proof needed for justification. So, no report, no expense check. I would simply ask the home office to send the individual's expense check to me instead of to the employee's home. And I would tell the person involved that I was holding it. I would say pleasantly, "I'm holding your expense check. Just as soon as I get your overdue reports, the check is yours." Childish? Perhaps, but surely as effective as the IRS. Did you ever hear of a refund without first submitting a proper tax return?

Let me hasten to assure you that too much importance can never be placed on reports. In addition to supplying you with vital information, they represent a method through which you keep a finger on the pulse of each member of your sales team. Therefore, you have every reason to become a stickler over getting them on time. In the long run you'll be glad you did, especially since you will soon discover that when an individual is having trouble getting reports to you on time, chances are that there are other problems, over and above that one, that require your serious attention. And the late reports may very well be like the tip of an iceberg, with much more below the surface. I found this to be the case in any number of instances during my sales manager days. One in particular, a most bizarre experience, still stands out in my mind, even though it took place quite some time ago. Here is what happened.

I had a better-than-average salesman in the Boston area who had been punctual in submitting reports over a period of better than three years. Then, as I left to go on vacation on the third of the month, I realized that Harold had not yet submitted his itinerary for that month. But this was so unusual for him that I didn't get concerned, particularly since I wouldn't be trying to contact him for the next two weeks while on vacation. I felt certain that it was probably in the mail. But it wasn't. When I checked my mail upon returning, I found cause for concern. Not only was Harold's itinerary still missing, but so was his monthly summary report for the previous month, which was due on the tenth. It was now the eighteenth, and I reached for the phone. No answer. I called several times that evening. Still no answer. Called at 7:00 A.M. the next morning and again at 7:30. No answer.

Harold was a bachelor in his late forties who lived in a small apartment in one of the nicer Boston suburbs. On my way into downtown Boston that day I stopped at his apartment building. His company car was in his assigned space. I went to the front door and peeked through the window in his mailbox. No mail. I pressed his button on the intercom board. No answer. Maybe he went out for breakfast and walked, I reasoned hopefully. Since I was meeting another salesman at 9:00, I had to leave, but not before placing one of my business cards in Harold's mailbox. On it I wrote, "Please phone me tonight. Very important."

I was home all evening. The call from Harold never came. As late as 11:30 I called *him*. Still no answer. Now I was puzzled. If Harold was out of town because of some emergency, he would have dropped me a note. Certainly he would have informed the home office. He had done neither. This was now a serious matter. So I made the decision that my mission for the next day would be to *find and talk to Harold.*

At 7:00 A.M. I was at his apartment building. His car was still in the parking lot. My calling card was no longer in his mailbox. He had to be around. Pressed his button on the intercom. He didn't answer. The next step was to knock on his door. But the lobby door was always locked. So I had to wait for someone to come out, and then I could slip in. Very shortly that happened, and I was now on the third floor. Just as I was about to knock on Harold's door, I heard his toilet flushing. Now I knew that he was inside. I knocked—several times. No answer. In a strong voice I said, "Harold, it's Paul. I must talk with you." Still no answer.

I had noticed an advertising flyer that someone had slipped under his door. One-third of it was still protruding. As I stood in the hallway pondering my next move, a heavyset man walked by. When his heavy footsteps on the rubber-matted wooden floor had faded away, I saw the flyer being retrieved from the inside. "How spooky," I thought. "Harold is in there and he thinks I've left. I'll knock again." As I did, I said, "Harold, I know you're in there. I just saw you pull in the advertisement under the door. Now, open up. It's important that we talk." No answer.

What happened next could have been part of a detective movie. The resident manager of the apartment building was not in, so there was no help to be had from him. I would have to resort to the police. The building was on a major thoroughfare. I no sooner came out of the front door than I saw a police cruising car. I flagged it down.

"Officer, an employee of mine lives in this building

alone. I have reason to believe he's in his apartment, but I can't get him to answer, and I'm worried about him. Can you help me?''

"Sure," he said, as he motioned to his partner to park the cruiser. After I explained my many attempts to communicate with Harold, the spokesman of the police duo said, "We'll get into his apartment through the fire escape by going through the apartment door next to his."

At the front door he pressed the button for the next-door apartment. A lady's voice came through the intercom: "Who is it?"

"This is the police. Please press the buzzer so we can get in. We need to speak with you." The lady couldn't have been more cooperative. She claimed that she hadn't seen Harold in several weeks and that it was okay to go through her apartment to reach the fire escape. When the rotund officer discovered that he didn't fit through any of the four small windows comprising the bay window, he asked if I would consider doing so. I agreed, went through the window onto the fire escape and over to Harold's window. It was open, but the shade was down. I lifted the shade and climbed in.

The apartment looked as if a cyclone had hit it. The bed was not made. Clothes were everywhere, as were drinking glasses, samples of our products, literature, forms, shoes, empty beer cans, and mail. But Harold didn't seem to be there. Really, now, I thought, where could he have gone? He was not in the kitchen or in the bathroom or under the bed. There was only one other possibility left—the bedroom closet. I opened the door, and there he was facing me, standing in his shorts and undershirt. He looked startled, but so was I! Neither of us said a word.

There was a pounding on the living-room door. It was the police officer shouting, "Is he all right?" I opened the door. "Yes, Officer, he's fine." By this time Harold had put on a robe. The officer looked at him and asked, "Will you be okay?"

"Yes, thank you," Harold answered. I thanked him, too, and he left.

Harold was visibly embarrassed and understandably so. We sat down, and I spoke first.

"Harold, I'm sorry I had to come into your apartment through the window. But I just had to see you. And you wouldn't communicate with me in any manner."

"I understand, Paul. I would have done the same thing had I been in your shoes." We had a long talk. There were no arguments. Harold realized that he owed me an explanation, and when we got to the end of it I learned that he had broken up with a girlfriend two months ago and couldn't get her off his mind. There was no chance of making up, since she had found someone else. He had been doing nothing except brooding, staying in his apartment, and drinking beer. And he had not covered his territory for over two months. Occasionally he had spent a few hours on the phone and picked up orders that way. The latter was a killer. That meant that he had falsified over forty daily reports. In all that time he had not made a sales call. And yet he had listed dozens of druggists and doctors on his daily call reports. Amazingly enough, he had been able to motivate himself to fill out falsified daily reports—but not to go out and cover his territory.

Naturally, I had mixed emotions. One had to feel sorry for someone in this state of romantic depression. But, on the other hand, he was mature enough to know what the world is all about. He was not a teen-ager whose terminated love affair could only be faced with contemplated suicide.

There was a big decision to be made. Is an attempt to

salvage Harold considered, or is he to be terminated for the good of the company and in deference to the firm's hard and fast rule that falsified call reports mean immediate dismissal? I could have consulted with the home office but decided against such a move. After all, if a district sales manager can't make decisions on his own, he's not a sales manager.

While Harold was dressing (so that we could go out for coffee and talk things over), I weighed the pros and cons very carefully and decided that, really, he had left me no choice. Two months of no territorial coverage without my being told was too much to accept, let alone the falsified reports. At the coffee shop I explained to Harold that I could sympathize with his personal problems but that regrettably, in view of his actions, I had to dismiss him from our employ. He took it as a mature adult would. He said that he expected nothing different.

Bizarre as this episode may have been, one thing is certain. The situation may have conceivably continued for another month or two had I not pounced on the late reports infraction as quickly as possible. Only two weeks later I had a new sales representative in Harold's territory who, in one year, increased sales by 40 percent.

Reports are very important, and when they are late, *immediate* action is *always* indicated.

Are Your Counseling Sessions Productive?

Remember the day you were working on territory with your newest salesman and he got into an argument with a prospective buyer? Remember how you couldn't wait to get outside so you could tell him exactly what he did wrong?

Remember how you explained that he had not handled the objections properly and that he was really not fully prepared to make that call? Then, when you got into the reasons why you should never argue with a prospect, a huge, noisy truck came by, and you ended up shouting at him?

The entire counseling session failed, didn't it? You knew it had failed because some of the same mistakes were made later on in the day. Because your salesman's attitude was not too good. And because no matter what you said at the end of the day, he just couldn't seem to perk up.

This is a problem that many sales managers get into without realizing it. Counseling sessions are certainly in order during field visits; however, unless they are handled properly, they will fail to produce the results desired. In this particular instance it was a complete mistake to try to have a counseling session on the sidewalk of a busy street. It's unprofessional, it's too noisy, it's within earshot of passersby, and it's never well accepted. You could argue that you wanted to discuss something while it was still fresh in your mind. If you had let it go until the end of the day, you could have forgotten.

Of course there is the alternative or jotting things down in your notebook and then bringing them up at the end of the day. But this is not a good idea either. As you jot things down, your sales representative will become apprehensive, wondering how bad things really are, and this certainly affects his or her confidence. Successive calls may be handled less effectively due to nervous tension.

The best way to handle the situation is for a sales manager to remember the important points during the morning to be discussed at lunch and during the afternoon to be discussed at the end of the day. And, incidentally, the good points should be remembered as well as the bad ones. If something happens during a sales call that requires immediate discussion, then it is better to return to the automobile and do so in complete privacy. If you decide to have a counseling session over lunch, here, too, there is some strategy to be used. There is nothing more frustrating than trying to have a decent conversation while a waitress or waiter continues to interrupt. First you're asked if there will be drinks, then if you have decided from the menu, then the food is delivered, then you are asked if there will be dessert, then the coffee is delivered, then the check, and so on. Counseling is important, and it should be taken seriously whenever it is attempted. Experience has shown that there can be as many as twelve interruptions by the restaurant staff in the course of a meal. How can anyone have a serious conversation under those circumstances? The answer is really simple: Don't try to counsel during the meal. Spend that time to get to know your people better. Answer questions about routines, forms, products, but don't get into anything heavy. Then, ask for a pot of coffee and the check. Pay the check, and this will conclude the transactions, and there will be no further interruptions. You can now have a meaningful counseling session.

At the end of the day, the car offers the needed privacy and quiet for counseling. But remember, we said that you should be looking for the good things as well as the bad. There's a good reason for this. Whenever you conduct a counseling session, always leave the good things for last. Certainly you should point out what was done wrong and follow that up immediately with how it should be done. But after the criticism, be sure that you come up with some compliments. You should always leave your people feeling good after a counseling session. No matter how critical you might have been, if you end up with some complimentary remarks, you will not affect the person's confidence or general attitude. And this is especially important after you have left at the completion of your field visit.

Much has been said as to exactly what should be accomplished during a field visit. All too often sales supervisors observe their people's performance from the standpoint of product knowledge, company policies, technical data, etc. While all of this is important, it should usually be secondary to the sales representative's selling ability. The field visit affords an excellent opportunity for on-the-job sales training. Much attention should be given to this. In the end, it's the selling skills that will bring home the sale. And since selling skills are not transmitted as well on paper as is other information, a sales supervisor should take advantage of field visits to demonstrate techniques whenever the occasion arises. I don't mean that in so doing you should do some selling for your people. Not at all. This would be a very bad supervisory move. You should never slip into the conversation unless asked to do so by the sales representative or the customer. And then you should get out promptly once the purpose has been served. Never take over the actual making of the sale. This has a very bad effect on both your salespeople and their customers.

It has been said that the field visit is one of the most important supervisory tools in the handling of outside salespeople because it affords the opportunity to conduct counseling sessions face to face. They are far superior to those conducted over the telephone or in writing. Yet, far too many sales managers are not particularly welcome on field visits just because their people dread the counseling sessions that are sure to come about.

Well, these sessions need not be dreaded by any stretch of the imagination. If conducted at the right time, in the right place, and under the proper guidelines, they can become an excellent give-and-take forum rather than scolding sessions that are long remembered.

The biggest compliment any of your people can pay you is when they tell you they wish you could work with them on territory more often—and mean it. At that point you know that you are handling the field visit, and the counseling sessions therein, properly.

3
Training

You have been told many times that the training of those who report to you is, in large measure, your responsibility. You have been reminded that you are in the best position to see that training takes place. After all, you are there—in the field—in regular contact with your people. But you still wonder, from time to time, just how much training should be done and how often.

Are you Training Too Much, Too Often?

Well, the answer to *how much* is easy. You should see that your people get as much training as is humanly possible. Why? Because no one in selling ever reaches the point where no further training is necessary. There is excellent proof for such a statement. Studies have shown that the human brain reaches its highest level of retention at age twenty-three. From then on, it's downhill all the way. Therefore, it's obvious that unless training is given on a continual basis, the benefits are soon lost due to the inability of the human brain to retain information for extended periods of time. Repetition is the only answer. On the average, of a message heard only once, we forget

64% in 24 hours
85% in 2 weeks
98% in 30 days

So, it becomes the constant task of the field sales manager to train, retrain, and continue to train indefinitely. The trick is to make it sound somewhat different each time. Using a varied approach, a different avenue, you repeatedly make the same important points over and over again. And you never let an opportunity slip by. For instance, you are spending a day on territory with a sales representative. All is going well. She is a seasoned saleswoman, has been with you for several years. But you notice that during one of the sales calls she asks for the order once, doesn't get it, and makes no further effort to close the sale. The opportunity is golden. The time is now. Just as soon as you return to her car, and while the sales interview is still very fresh in mind, you review with her the time-tested selling technique that spells out that you always ask for the order a minimum of three times.

Yes, this goes for experienced salespeople as well as the newly hired ones. Sometimes, those who are quite experienced tend to forget the basics through which they achieved success originally and begin to drift. So, they need just as much training as anyone else.

Then there is the problem of *how often* should you train. Obviously, the answer is exactly the same as for *how much*. You train as often as is humanly possible. You seize every opportunity and you devise ways and means through which to bring constant training about. For instance. Each time that you hire a new individual for your field staff, the procedure in most companies is to send that person to the home office for basic training. A great deal of this training will be on product knowledge, but a substantial amount of sales training is usually also included. And the new hiree comes back to the field loaded with enthusiasm, knowledge, and vigor. It's always a joy to observe this. Well, how about extending this to the rest of your field staff? Why not get copies of what was used during this home office training. Then distribute the material to all of your people. Attach a note. Explain that you want to keep everyone up to date on what's going on regarding training at the home office. It makes them all feel more informed, and in the process they are getting additional training.

But that's not enough, of course. Hold as many sales meetings as your budget will allow. At every one of these meetings, do some training. At least 50 percent of a meeting should be devoted to training. And between meetings you always have the opportunity to do some training on an individual basis during field visits.

Now, field visit training should not be done on a "let's see what happens" basis. Decide in advance of the visit what weaknesses in that particular individual you will work on. Bring along any materials that will help you make an impact while administering the training and never leave without reviewing what was covered during the visit. If the individual you are about to visit has no significant weaknesses, then be sure to ask about any problems that are being encountered. Do this during a counseling session and apply whatever training will help in the solving of the problems.

Above all, keep all training positive. Never tell your

people what they are doing wrong without telling or showing the right way. Some managers feel that making people come up with the right way on their own forces them to think and makes more of an impact. This may be true sometimes and with some people. But the fact remains that under such strategy the manager is always negative, always critical, always finding fault. In the process a poor image is developed, field visits are despised rather than welcomed, and the training is far from effective.

Is the Training Being Digested?

You are fully aware of the importance of training and you give as much as possible to your field staff. Yet, over and over again you find evidence of shoddiness in sales calls, inattention to important details, etc. You wonder how this is possible. After all the training that has been given on these very matters, how can people fall so short of the mark?

Well, the answer usually lies in the fact that a great deal of training is not digested. It is certainly accepted when given. But it is far from thoroughly digested. The solution is to force-feed. You must force the digestion of training material by requiring feedback. It's the same as in communications. You never know whether or not you have thoroughly communicated with someone until you get a response that proves you've gotten through. In training, however, we forget that all too often. For instance, you send out a sales bulletin to all of your people. In it you may make an important training point or two. You then assume that everyone *(a)* will read it; *(b)* will understand it; and *(c)* is able to apply the information. Even though *(a)* and *(b)* may be assumed, based on knowing your own salespeople well, *(c)* cannot. The only insurance is feedback. By asking each recipient, in the very content of the sales bulletin, to send back a short note explaining how the information will be—or has been—applied, you will insure proper digestion.

A few years ago a client company of ours decided to purchase audio-cassette players for all of its salespeople so that tapes could be listened to while traveling in their cars. Then they purchased "off the shelf" training tapes and distributed them, one each month, to the field staff. After a few months, at a manager's meeting, it was learned that the tapes were not being digested. While most of the sales staff were aware of the contents, the techniques were not being put to use. We were asked for a solution to the problem and came up with this variation. We customized a series of short tapes in which we married some Lacy selling techniques to specific products that they manufactured. Then we buried in each the statement "Please send your district manager a short note explaining what happened when you used this technique." The result was unbelievable. Everyone listened to the tapes, *everyone* replied with notes, and sales increased substantially.

This problem of digestion must also be kept in mind during classroom-type training at sales meetings. To lecture or show visuals is not enough. There must be participation of the feedback type. Get people to mouth examples of what you have been teaching, or give a quiz on the material covered. Even a single statement on how each point made "applies to my territory or customers," requested in writing—right there on the spot—will do much toward proper digestion of training material.

Is the New Trainee Lagging Behind?

You hired Bill French three months ago and you were thoroughly convinced that he would make a great addition to your staff. Just out of college, with excellent marks, he looked and acted like a salesman, and everyone at the home office told you that you had made an excellent choice. But now, three months later, his sales are lagging far behind quota. You know that he's trying and that he's making the calls. But he simply isn't meeting with much success.

Do you begin to consider the possibility of replacing him? Not really. Generally this would be far too early for that.

More often than not the problem is centered around training. You may feel that you have spent a generous amount of your time on territory with him. And what about the two weeks he spent at the home office training class? you ask. Sure, he's received a substantial amount of training—but how much of it has been *sales training*? At best it was no more than 50 percent. His head has been filled with product knowledge, company policies, forms, reports, and a myriad of other details.

Now, let's step back and take a good, hard look at the big picture. Bill had done well in college. His excellent marks proved that. But what had he studied? Languages, sciences, art, music? Even if he graduated from the business school of a large university, his major courses most likely consisted of economics, market research, accounting, and sales management. Perhaps a smattering of salesmanship—but far from enough. Of the thousands of colleges and universities scattered throughout the fifty states in this country, only two institutions offer salesmanship as a major subject. These are the state university at Memphis, Tennessee, and Lansing Community College in Lansing, Michigan, which offers an associate degree with a major in salesmanship. So there you are. The problem is clear. In the one subject that would further his success the most—salesmanship—Bill has received the least training.

The solution, therefore, is obvious. In order to salvage Bill, you must get as much *sales training* into him as is humanly possible and as quickly as possible. How can this be done? Well, to begin with, a counseling session is necessary. Explain the problem to him and ask for his cooperation in solving it. Point out that he must spend one to two hours each evening in the study of salesmanship—more on weekends. Then supply him with the study materials.

If your company has a sales training manual, start with it. Outline a schedule of study for Bill based on the manual and have him submit completed tests to you at specified times. If tests on the manual are not available to you, develop quizzes yourself. If you don't have time to do so, assign the task to one of your experienced salespeople. That individual will gain personally by doing so.

When that phase has been completed, start Bill on a book-reading phase. There are well over two thousand books on salesmanship registered at the Library of Congress. Every neighborhood library has one or two dozen of these on the shelves. Select four of the better-known and have Bill read one per week. Have him submit to you a written report of what he learned from each book and how he plans to apply it.

While he is reading books, you should obtain for him a prepackaged sales course. Then you present it to him when he submits his last book report. Make sure that you set a deadline date by which the course must be completed.

During the time that all of this is going on, you will notice a steady increase in Bill's sales. As he grasps more and more of the selling techniques to which he is being exposed, he makes more sales. Many of these techniques may well have been covered during his home office training. But too much was thrown at him at one time, and not enough was retained.

I realize that all of this requires much follow-through on your part. And it also requires your spending as much time on territory with Bill as you possibly can—to encourage him and to make sure that he is applying what he is learning. However, the rewards will be far beyond your expectations. Soon he will no longer be lagging behind in sales. Instead he will be blossoming out as a very effective member of your sales staff whom you salvaged from a potential disaster.

Are Your Salespeople Training Themselves?

It is sometimes annoying, if not outright exasperating, when one member of your sales staff calls you and extols the virtues of a motivational audio tape that he happened to obtain. He has been listening to it for a few days, is very excited about it, and wants to tell you of its contents. Then, right after you hang up, the phone rings again, and it's another of your salespeople, who read an article on selling in a trade journal and wants you to know all about it. Your immediate reaction to these calls is not too good. Not only are they time-consuming for you, but you have to listen intently in order to compare the material to what is being used by your company. You want to make sure that your people are not straying from the well-established patterns of training set forth within your organization.

The reason behind your reaction is not solid. In fact, the situation is not a problem at all. In the first place, it is totally impossible to keep blinders on your people. There is no way through which to insure that they are trained only by you and your company. They are bound to come in contact with sales training materials, books and articles on selling, etc., as they travel within their territories. But what's wrong with that? The more that their eyes are opened to the many avenues that lead to success in the art of convincing, the better. You want your product or service sold—to as many people as possible and in the largest possible amounts. Does it matter *how* it's sold? If it's done ethically, with the proper moral standards, does it really matter *how*?

Whether we like to admit this or not, every individual who sells develops his or her own style of selling. If you took any two people with the exact same backgrounds and who had never sold before and gave them the very same type and amount of sales training, the end result would differ in each case. Since all salespeople sell through their individual personalities and since no two people have the exact same personality, something happens along the way. Yes, the material learned is the same, but when it's put to use through one's personality, it comes out differently.

But, I repeat, does it really matter *how* they sell? This is a hang-up that many companies have created into a monster. Hundreds of times, as I've discussed training programs with client companies, I have heard one or more of these statements uttered with conviction:

- Our product line is unique!
- This company's sales staff is unique!
- Our method of distribution is unique!
- Our training methods are unique!
- Our sales meetings are unique!

Every company feels that they do things differently. Their own way is the best way. The competitor is all wet. Anything he does is wrong. Now, there is nothing radically wrong with this attitude, unrealistic as it may be. It really reflects a super ego or an unfounded pride of authorship. But so be it. We all know that a certain amount of egotism helps in salesmanship. However, why restrain an individual from becoming better at his profession by limiting him to only that training and only that knowledge that is generated within the company? When a salesman makes himself better by adding to what his company gives him in the way of training, he sells more. When he sells more, his manager looks better, and the company prospers.

So, what should you do with explorers who seek training on their own? Encourage them to do so. The more, the better. In fact, get even more mileage out of this phenomenon. Whenever one of your people tells you about an extra sales book read or an extra sales course taken, first extend the deserved compliments and then schedule that person to make a presentation on the material learned at your very next sales meeting. I can guarantee you that whatever the material is, it can be applied to your *unique* operation. How can I guarantee it?

For the past fifteen years I have been making over one hundred speeches each year on salesmanship. All of them have imparted Lacy selling techniques. And of the thousands of salespeople in those audiences, from all types of industries, not *one* has ever come to me to say that something I included just didn't apply. When you consider that the person who will be billed for my fee is almost always in the audience, you can readily see how the statement can be guaranteed.

4
Sales Meetings

In general you may have felt that the last sales meeting you held went over well. At least that's what your salespeople told you. But when you analyzed all of its aspects, you came to the conclusion that the location was wrong. You made the decision that you would never go back to that hotel with a meeting.

Is the Location Wrong?

Having been a guest speaker at over one-thousand sales meetings, I can assure you that there are many hotels that have proved to have been the wrong location. I can also assure you that many sales managers didn't realize that they were conducting a meeting in the wrong location. What do we mean by the "wrong location"? Well, here are a few examples:

- The hotel that gives you part of their main ballroom, which is divided into a number of meeting rooms by sliding doors. I have yet to find sliding doors, whether folding or otherwise, that are capable of keeping out noise from an adjacent section. It seems that there is always a speaker in the next section with an extremely loud voice or is using a microphone with volume that's too high or is showing a motion picture with the projector's volume on the highest number.
- The meeting room that overlooks the hotel pool, where there is a host of bikini-clad, curvaceous beauties sunning themselves—and there are no drapes.
- The meeting room in a coastal resort hotel with picture windows, allowing a breathtaking view of the boats that constantly come by.
- The hotel located right in the center of town with inadequate parking facilities, making it almost impossible for attendees to get rid of their automobiles—the main reason why the meeting was thirty minutes late getting started and the whole agenda was knocked out of kilter.
- The meeting room located right next to the parking garage, where horns are blowing all day long to warn against a blind corner.
- The hotel that has no facilities for serving coffee in a foyer or hallway, and the waiter comes into the meeting room twenty minutes prior to the coffee break to set up and disrupts the entire meeting in the process.
- The meeting room located directly across the hall from a bank of elevators, whose bells ring all day every time elevators reach that level.

- The hotel that has only been opened three or four weeks and whose bugs have still not been taken out of its operation. Everything seems to go wrong. Nothing happens on schedule.
- The meeting room that does not have its own thermostat for air-conditioning purposes or whose thermostat has been carefully locked so that no one can touch it. (It is important to have access to a thermostat in order to make the room comfortable and govern its ventilation, particularly if there is much smoking going on.)
- The hotel that promises to supply you with a chalkboard and has no chalk or erasers to go with it.

The solution to these problems is simply this: Make a complete checklist for yourself that includes all of the situations listed, as well as any others that you may have encountered. Then, when arranging for the meeting room with the manager of a particular hotel, take the list along with you and check off all of the possibilities before agreeing to the rental of a particular room. But even then, you must go one step further. Don't let the hotel function manager convince you that their policy is to assign meeting rooms, specifically by room number, the day before the meetings are held—sometimes even on the morning of the meeting. You must have the option of selecting the particular room you want—one that fits your specific needs and that remains yours for that day under any circumstances. If that assurance cannot be given you, then go to another hotel. Sales meetings are too costly and too important to have them adversely affected by the very location in which they are held.

Are Interruptions Annoying?

How annoyed you were at one of your recent sales meetings when it seemed that every time an important point was being made an interruption came about. This was so annoying to you that you said to yourself, "There must be a way of conducting a sales meeting without interruptions of any kind." There is.

For openers, you must make sure that no one, I repeat, no one, is allowed the flexibility of entering your meeting room at will. There are only two ways to accomplish this, and the first way is the best.

1. Place a member of the office staff outside the door of your meeting room, in the corridor. This person can be set up with a table and chair, can distribute literature and name badges, can take and deliver messages, etc. But the most important function of this person is to make sure that once the meeting starts, no one is allowed to enter the meeting room. In other words, this person becomes the master-at-arms for the duration of the meeting.

2. When the above arrangement is not possible, appoint an individual who is attending the meeting as master-at-arms, and ask this individual to take a seat just inside the door to the meeting room. If someone opens the door, this individual is to immediately go outside the room and hold a conversation in the corridor to discover what the reason for the interruption is.

This type of insulation will guarantee that interruptions do not come about. You have probably experienced, in many hotels, the lost soul who opens the door and looks in—only to realize with astonishment that he has entered the wrong room. Sometimes interruptions are of an even brasher nature. I have experienced all types of interruptions while making a speech, and all of them were attributable to poor planning. How well I recall that evening in upstate New York when I was the featured speaker at the closing banquet of a sales meeting of a very large company. I was making a very dramatic point. I had lowered my voice substantially and was hugging the microphone. You could have heard a pin drop. And right in the middle of that particular sequence the back door of the motel meeting room swung open and a well-corseted waitress with a booming voice screamed, "Is there anyone in here driving a blue Chevrolet? It's blocking the delivery entrance." There was a hush. The Chevrolet belonged to no one in the room. The train of thought had been broken. Sure, I recovered. I smiled and said that she was training to become an opera star. They laughed. But what happened to the dramatic point. I went back to pick it up, but it wasn't anywhere near as dramatic.

Why should this be allowed to happen? When you pay good money for a meeting room, when you spend hours planning for success, why should a waitress or anyone else be allowed to barge in and interrupt you at a crucial point in the meeting? Interruptions can be avoided. You must plan their avoidance. And, oh, yes, there is one other interrupter: the telephone. The best way to silence the phone is to take the receiver off the cradle and then, to make sure that no one arbitrarily replaces it, scotch-tape the receiver to the wall. Only then does it become obvious that you do not want the phone in operation. Oh, I know, you can argue that this is too drastic. You could easily call the hotel operator and leave word that this extension is not to be rung. However, that doesn't work. First of all, what happens to people internally who dial the wrong number and ring your meeting room? Also, the operator may forget. Or when the operator goes home at 3:00 P.M. and the relief operator comes in, the message is not transmitted. And you become vulnerable all over again. It just isn't worth it.

But what about the phone calls from the home office, you say? They'll just have to wait until the next day. Most emergencies are not emergencies at all. And let's not forget, the sales meeting has an important function. Why ruin it with pseudoemergencies, with messages that easily could have waited.

What is Your Goal?

Your national sales manager decided to attend your meeting. He was making a swing through the general area and thought this would be a great time to attend your sales meeting and also get to know more of the people in your district or branch. At the end of the meeting he shakes your hand, compliments you, and says something like, "In general it was a good meeting." You quickly catch on to the "in general" and you say, "Do you have any suggestions as to how it could have been made better?" And he says, "Yes, the agenda was a little weak. It could have been a lot stronger by giving the whole meeting a theme."

Ah, yes. A theme for the meeting. There should always be a theme. There should always be a purpose. It's absolutely nonsensical when companies have sales meetings, say, every quarter, just because it's time to have a sales meeting. Those meetings are usually far from successful.

They're put together haphazardly; there's no real reason for the meeting—and it shows.

Whether the meeting is automatically scheduled for a certain time of the year or whether it has been called to bring a specific message before the sales team, the setting up of the agenda should be given scientific thought.

Begin with what should be the end result. Write that down. What is to be accomplished by the end of the meeting? Then you work back as to how to reach that goal before the meeting is concluded. What is the input? What are the convincing factors that will bring about the goal? As you write down all of these factors, you can, if you look hard enough, see the thread of the theme. Nail it down and make it creative. For instance:

- *We grow through knowledge.* This would make a good theme when the meeting is designed to get salespeople to study literature more carefully and become more knowledgeable of products, especially when the products are highly scientific in nature.
- *Second effort.* When sales are not meeting expectations, and it seems clear that salesmen are not trying hard enough. The thrust of the meeting is on making that second effort, that extra call, attaining a never-say-die attitude.
- *There's safety in numbers.* A possible theme when it is apparent that your people are not making as many sales calls as you expect. The thrust is on the fact that the more sales calls, the more chances of making sales.
- *Nothing happens until somebody sells something.* A great theme through which a sales force is made to feel very important. The idea to get across is that absolutely nothing happens to the economy until

salespeople go out, make sales calls, move products, and maintain people in the factories in their jobs.

- *Sell with personality.* A theme revolving around the personality traits of people who sell and what they should do to make their personalities more sales oriented.

Once a theme has been developed, it should be promoted strongly. For instance, the meeting announcement should have the theme at the top of the page. Any announcements regarding the meeting in a house organ should have, as the headline, the theme of the meeting. At the meeting itself, on the wall behind the speaker's rostrum, place a large banner with the theme lettered on it in bright colors. Place smaller banners containing the theme on the other walls of the meeting room so that they are visible from every possible angle. If notebooks or pads are distributed for the taking of notes, make sure that the theme is clearly displayed on them.

When you open the meeting, make sure that the goal of the meeting is defined at the very beginning, and in the process explain the origin and significance of the theme. During the meeting refer to the theme as often as you possibly can. And at the close of the meeting explain what was done to reach the goal outlined at the beginning of the meeting, associate everything that happened with the theme, and the very closing statements of the meeting should be the mouthing of the theme itself.

This is what makes a strong agenda. You see, the agenda might be fairly strong on its own by the very fact of the importance of the subjects covered, but without a theme as a thread to hold the whole program together there is always the possibility that the meeting will turn out to be a hodgepodge, and, as a result, the attendees, or a visiting dignitary, will walk away feeling that there was a weak agenda to the meeting.

One final thought on the subject: No sales meeting should ever be considered to have a good agenda without some sales training having been included. Always look for a way to interject sales training, no matter what the theme of the meeting may be.

Is the Home Office Speaker Boring?

You were planning a sales meeting and you got the word from the home office that Mr. E. B. Jones, the vice-president for personnel, would like to be included in the agenda. He wants to bring to the attention of members of the sales staff the details in connection with fringe benefits. You have no choice but to include him in the agenda and you allot to him the thirty minutes suggested.

At the meeting his appearance is almost a disaster. Everything was going well, momentum was being gained with each segment of the agenda, all in attendance were very enthusiastic (they seemed to be enjoying every minute of it), and then, for a change of pace, Jones approached the lectern. He opened his thick file folder and with a horrendous monotone proceeded to read some of the driest material ever. He talked about the retirement plan, profit sharing, the stock purchasing plan, and the suggestion system. Finally, to put the finishing touches on his speech, he went into the maternity insurance program and then the gory details of the coverage for accidents. If you lose one eye and one limb, you get x dollars; if you lose two limbs, you get x dollars; if you lose both eyes, you get *x* dollars; etc., etc., etc. What's even worse, he took fifty minutes instead of his allotted thirty. By the time he was through, most of your people were yawning, all of them were thoroughly bored, and you had developed a new ulcer.

Is there a solution to this? There certainly is, and it lies well within your power. First of all, let's understand that the only people from the home office who can lend stature to your meeting or contribute substantially to it are the president of the company, the executive vice-president, the vice-president for sales and/or marketing, and the national sales manager. That's it. Individuals from the financial, manufacturing, quality control, and other departments are to be avoided whenever possible. On occasion, however, someone at the home office decides that there should be some representation out in the field by some of these individuals. Many times it's simply a case of giving them a *trip* for morale purposes. And you, as the "benefactor," end up suffering for it. And one thing is certain, most of the individuals who fall in this category are generally poor public speakers. Not only do they bring a prepared speech typed in large letters, but they are so inexperienced and so nervous at the lectern that they spit all over themselves trying to read it. You don't need this at your sales meeting.

When you are *asked* to invite such a person to your meeting, you can easily overcome this request by stating that the agenda is so tight, because of so much *training*, that you really can't see your way clear to make room for a guest speaker. You will not be lying. You should have a tight agenda, and it should be jam-packed with as much training as possible. Usually this explanation will be accepted. In fact, you will be thought of even more highly for placing so much emphasis on training which, of course, brings in more sales.

When you are told that Mr. Jones will be a speaker at your meeting and you have no choice, your only alternative is to explain emphatically that you can allow only ten minutes for this presentation because of a jam-packed agenda—filled with training. And when the home office representative arrives, make it quite clear that only ten minutes can be allotted to the subject. Then when the presentation has gone ten minutes, stand up and walk toward the podium. Stand beside him if you have to. Make it clear that time is up. Assert yourself. It's your meeting. If the speaker is somewhat disgruntled, you may rest assured that your superior will always back you up.

The theory here is, of course, that ten minutes—no matter how boring—cannot cause you that much harm. And by the way, the night before the meeting, when you welcome the guest speaker to your home base, ask him if he has timed his presentation, to make sure that it is within ten minutes. That's for insurance purposes.

Is Participation Enthusiastic?

You had convinced yourself that the next sales meeting was going to be different. At that sales meeting you were going to get an awful lot of participation. You were going to make everybody in attendance feel that they were part of the meeting. But it just didn't happen. You wondered why. After all, you asked for questions. Nobody had any. You asked if anyone wanted to add to what had already been said. Nobody did. You asked if anyone disagreed with what had been said. Nobody did. It was like holding a meeting in a wax museum. The figures were totally inanimate.

It didn't have to be that way. Participation is important in *all* meetings. It stimulates those in attendance and makes everyone feel a part of what's going on. Even those who don't participate get that feeling. But participation can only be attained by design. You can almost decide on exactly how much you're going to get at a sales meeting.

You do this by *scheduling* the participation. For instance, there is no better training than that which is gained through role-playing. This is when you assign one of your salespeople the task of acting as a buyer and another to act as the sales representative. No one ever minds being the buyer. Yet, they always mind being the sales rep. The reason is obvious. It is usually very difficult, in the presence of your peers, to make a sales presentation that is not very refined. Why isn't it refined? Because poeple who sell have a reputation of not being terribly organized. Most of them like to fly by the seat of their pants. They don't make up a presentation well in advance. They learn the product, everything that it will do. And then, in the presence of the prospect, play it by ear. You can be sure, however, that when asked to make a presentation at the sales meeting, in the presence of other members of the district sales staff, they wouldn't dare play it by ear. Simply stated, they don't want to make fools of themselves. They want to sound very professional and very organized. What a marvelous opportunity to make people organize their presentations. Particularly when you've noted, when working with them out in the field, that they simply are not organized enough. Those are the people that you appoint to play the role of "sales representative" in the role-playing session as part of your sales meeting.

This not only helps those in attendance, but it certainly helps the individual who must be prepared to do a professional job.

Some field sales managers always select their better salespeople to make such presentations. They rationalize that, in so doing, the expertise developed by the better people is transmitted to those who are not as good at selling a particular product. This theory is hard to argue with, but it should be extended to some degree. Extended to the point that one presentation per product just isn't enough at a sales meeting. It is really far better to first have a presentation by someone who hasn't been doing a good job on a specific product and then have the "expert" make a presentation on the very same product. This allows for comparison, as well as a jolt to the individual who prepared frantically (usually the night before) to do that professional job and at the meeting, when all this transpires, he realizes that he wasn't as good as he thought he was going to be. This makes him work harder.

At the conclusion of each role-playing session, the presentation should be critiqued by those in attendance. Make certain, however, that you announce that such criticism should always be of a constructive nature. You'll find that even the quietest of salespeople will jump in and make a significant comment under such circumstances.

Another way to promote participation is get individuals to prepare a presentation on subjects like:

- How to interject enthusiasm in your sales presentation
- How to handle the price buyer
- How to minimize the cost and magnify the returns

- How to overcome common objections on certain products
- How to qualify a prospect
- How to do more prospecting
- How to better manage territorial time

As you can see, these are very generalized topics and you can add a substantial number to those already listed that will fit into your operation. In each case, however, you have done a very important thing. You have forced the person who is charged with making the talk to research the subject, think about it creatively, come up with some intelligent ideas, and in the process become better in that area for it.

Still another way to bring about participation by design is to schedule brainstorming periods. Perhaps one in the morning and one in the afternoon. These are very simple to conduct. You announce, for instance, that there is going to be a brainstorming session on a particular subject. Announce this just before it is about to happen, without giving anyone a chance to give it serious thought or come up with negative ideas. Before proceeding you announce the ground rules. And they are simple. Explain that you are going to conduct a brainstorming session, which means that people in attendance should come up with as many ideas as possible that cross their minds in connection with the subject at hand. It doesn't matter whether the idea sounds reasonable or not. Also, no one in the group is to pooh-pooh an idea or counteract it with a negative remark, such as, "It can't be done." Then you go to the chalkboard, and as people raise their hands with ideas, you write it on the board. You refuse no ideas. You accept them all and write them all. At the end of the session, when the entire chalkboard has been filled, you go over them only from the standpoint of numbering them in order of their importance. That's all. None of them are erased from the board and none of them are disqualified. The list of subjects that can be used for brainstorming sessions at sales meetings is endless. Here are just a few of them:

- The benefits of a particular product
- Different ways of promoting a product
- How to make more calls
- Time-saving techniques
- Follow-up techniques

It is absolutely amazing how involved your people will become during a brainstorming session. They will enjoy the creativity that evolves from it. One big suggestion, however. Always appoint one of the people in attendance as the "scorekeeper." Have that person write on a sheet of paper everything that you write on the chalkboard. You can see the wisdom of this. When the session is all over and you erase the chalkboard, you will still have a record of what was said for further study and possible use of the ideas.

Yes, participation is easy to come by. You must simply plan for it, include it in your agenda, assign it, promote it, and then sit back and enjoy it. Remember, no matter how good a public speaker you consider yourself to be, it is very difficult to hold the attention of people for an entire day (even for half a day) without a break in the action in the form of participation. Besides, when people go to a sales meeting and never have an opportunity to speak, they come away feeling that it was a lecture. The feeling is then carried further to the point that maybe they were talked down to, handled as children. There is so much to be lost under those circumstances. And so much to be gained when participation is prevalent.

Are Visuals Effective?

So often you spend so much time and effort on visuals to stress important points at sales meetings and also to add some pizzazz. But instead of impressing the attendees you end up rather disgruntled because you continue to hear statements such as, "I can't see the numbers, what does that say in the upper right-hand corner? Which is the *red* line on the graph?"

This problem is usually caused by having visuals that look great when they are being prepared but that do not do the job when shown in a large room.

The most common offender at sales meetings is the overhead projector. This is the type that is placed on a small table, has a lighted platform on which transparencies or typed sheets are placed, and, through an adjustable lens (some two feet above the platform), projects the material by the use of mirrors, onto the wall or a screen. Like many other things, it is only as effective as the material being placed on the platform. Typewritten sheets are very ineffective. The size of the type is too small. No matter how far away from the wall it is being projected, it can rarely be read from the back of the room. If projected to very large proportions, it becomes so fuzzy that it simply cannot be understood. The discussion leader, who is standing beside the projector feeding the materials to it, can see everything on the screen quite plainly. But if someone is fifteen, twenty, thirty feet behind the location of the projector, viewing such visuals becomes a problem.

For all practical purposes, the overhead projector should be shied away from. For the reasons already covered, it is a constant source of problems. However, if you insist on using it, or another participant has transparencies that can only be used on this type of projector, it is strongly recommended that during such a presentation the people from the center of the room to the rear be asked to come forward, even if they have to stand during that presentation, in order that everyone can see exactly what is being projected. If you can get on the scene prior to the transparencies being made, try very hard to see that the lettering is at least five times the size of normal typewriter type. Only then can you hope for visibility and understanding by your audience.

The same theory must be carried over to flip charts. There is always that tendency to prepare flip charts in advance of the meeting. Why not? This makes it very easy. It gives the presenter an outline of his talk, so that stumbling is pretty much eliminated, and it allows for better comprehension because they are seeing it and hearing it at the same time. Flip charts have their problems too. If there is too much on one page or the lettering is too small, there is the problem of visibility. But there is also the problem of graphics. Most sales managers who prepare their own flip charts are far from good artists. This results in amateurish artwork, lines that are not straight, colors that don't blend with each other, etc. All of this produces a devastating effect. The real purpose of a flip chart is lost. As each page is flipped, the mind of the viewer goes to how poorly the graphics are or how hard it is to read it or how amateurish the whole thing looks, rather than listening to what is being said or absorbing what is being seen.

What's the answer? Certainly no one is implying that a flip chart needs to be prepared by an artist or an advertising agency every time you plan to use one. Far from it. The use of a flip chart still has its place under any circumstances. However, it is better to start off with a flip chart that has nothing on it and write on each page with a marking device as you go along with your presentation. Now, under these circumstances, you needn't worry about poor lettering, lines that are not straight, or any amount of sketching that you might want to attempt. The reason this is better is because they see it happening before their own eyes and, being engrossed in what's being said, much less attention is given to the graphics. Besides, they know that you're not an artist and they don't expect perfection in that area. With a prepared flip chart it could be assumed that it was done by a "two-bit" artist or that you did it yourself and didn't spend too much time on it.

Having conducted sales meetings for over twenty-five years, I still feel one of the finest visuals is the chalkboard. This is now called the chalkboard rather than a blackboard because not all of them are black. You have probably noticed that they come in green, brown, and even white. They are equally effective, provided that you use the right color chalk on them. White chalk, of course, always makes the blackboard look best; use yellow chalk on a brown or green chalkboard. And any of the dark-colored chalks, such as black, dark blue, dark green, purple, and dark brown, show up well on the white chalkboard.

There are so many reasons why a chalkboard is effective. To name a few:

- It is subliminally accepted as a teaching implement.
- It is readily available almost anywhere.
- It is easy to make changes or substitutions by erasing quickly.
- It can be moved around easily and placed where the lighting is best for all concerned.

But here is some important advice regarding the size of the chalk: In an average room in which fifty to seventy-five people are seated, using chalk of the average size is adequate. However, once there are more than seventy-five people, the need for larger chalk becomes very apparent. There is white chalk on the market (and several colors, too) that is approximately three-quarters of an inch in diameter. Some is available at one inch. Using chalk of these diameters will correspondingly increase the size of the impressions made on a chalkboard. Obviously, this vastly increases visibility.

Does the Projector Work?

You rented a motivational motion picture on which the promotion thoroughly convinced you that it would have a good impact at your sales meeting. You gave it a big buildup in your meeting announcement flyer, you placed the banners all over the room with the title of the film printed on them, and you followed through on all the other promotional bits per the instructions that came with the film. You had great expectations. But they all went down the drain. The projector wouldn't work.

You blamed everybody for this. The audiovisual dealer from whom you rented the projector (if it is a rented one) or the last person who used it or the person who brought it up to the meeting room for you and set it down rather carelessly.

But all of this could have been avoided, and should have been, by you. First of all, there is an unwritten rule about showing movies. You always have a dry run prior to the showing. This means setting up well in advance of the time that the meeting is to be held or even the night before and actually checking out the projector as well as seeing the motion picture. Seeing the motion picture is important because, while all of the promotion might be impressive, the motion picture may not be exactly what you want, or for that matter, it may even contradict certain of your company policies. So see it first. See it in advance of the meeting and even before you promote it if that's possible. Many companies who rent films will allow you to preview them in advance of a meeting. That, of course, is ideal. But, failing that, you must still take a good look at it before the meeting begins.

Then there is the projector to be contended with. Believe it or not, most projectors don't go on the blink that easily. Brand-name projectors have been carefully engineered for long-lasting performance. It is extremely rare when something goes wrong. What can, and many times does, happen is that the projection lamp burns out. So, you must never, never, never, try to show a motion picture without a spare projection lamp on the scene. It's like a spare tire. You wouldn't drive anywhere important without a spare tire in your car, would you? The same is true with a motion picture projector. You never know when the projection lamp will burn out on you. Most of them are good for twenty-five hours of use. But that means virtually nothing. A projection lamp is so delicate and it operates at such intensive heat that its life is not that predictable. Besides, most people do not follow the cardinal rule of projector operation. You see, there are two positions on the knob that turn the projector on and off. The first position activates the fan, and the second position turns on the projection lamp. After a film showing you should never turn off a projector by clicking both positions off at once. First you should turn off the projection lamp and hold the fan on for a few minutes. This allows proper cooling of the projection lamp and extends its life considerably.

So problems with projectors can, many times, be avoided. And they certainly should. After all, we have said that a sales meeting is important. And if it is important, it should not be interrupted or its pace slowed down to a crawl by audiovisual equipment that does not operate properly. Much of what has been said about a motion picture projector also applies to a slide projector, regardless of its type. Only when you have tested out the equipment, made sure that the proper slides are in place and in sequence, that none are upside down, etc., can you be sure that the problems will not arise.

It is a known fact that audiovisuals can spruce up a meeting substantially. But if something goes wrong in the course of their use, you will usually come to the conclusion that you would have been much better off without them. This is an area that certainly requires and deserves your close attention to detail.

5
Motivation

As a field sales manager, you consider yourself a good motivator. You are able to stimulate people. Especially at sales meetings you are able to spark a tremendous amount of enthusiasm among your salespeople. Yet, there is one member of your group who simply doesn't get excited. Ronald simply doesn't respond to motivation, you say. He's an average salesman, a plodder, one who takes responsibility seriously, but you can feel it in your bones that he will never be a *great* salesman. The reason? He can't be motivated.

Is Your Staff Motivated?

If in your entire sales staff you have just one individual who can't be motivated, you can consider yourself quite lucky. More often than not, in any group of twenty or more people there will be two or three who seem regularly to fail to respond to any and all efforts aimed at motivation. Why is that? Is it the way these particular individuals are constituted? Or is it because their leader has given up on them?

The latter is the more valid reason. You see, motivation is much like salesmanship. We all agree that no two people buy a product or service for the very same reason. We also agree that to sell an individual in the easiest and best possible way, we must find that person's dominant desire, the "Hot Button," to build our sales presentation around it. So, motivation is not that much different. If no two people buy a product or service for the very same reason, why should any two people be motivated in the exact same way? We are all individuals. We all respond to certain situations differently. And this is the very key to the entire subject of motivation.

Motivational forces to which people respond are as follows:

- Acceptance. (They want assurance that they are needed.)
- Accomplishment. (They derive pleasure from seeing a task completed.)
- Environment. (They greatly enjoy pleasant surroundings and friendly associates.)
- Recognition. (They thrive on praise and publicity.)
- Responsibility. (They like authority and discharge it well.)
- Security. (They are concerned about the future.)
- Status. (They are keenly aware of and impressed with status symbols.)

As you can see, these motivational forces cover a spectrum that's quite varied. As you look them over, you can almost pinpoint in your own mind which of your salespeople respond to which of these motivational forces. But sometimes we assume altogether too much in this area. We assume, for instance, that one individual is greatly motivated by one particular motivational force when actually it's a completely different force that is much more dominant. It becomes apparent, therefore, that to motivate people on a regular basis requires that we find each individual's Motivational Hot Button. Then, once you have found a person's MHB, you know exactly what has to be done to motivate that particular individual.

Of course, the next question is, how do you find an individual's MHB? Certainly you don't come out and ask for it outright. And to decide to wait for the time when it surfaces on its own is not wise. It could take a lot longer than you bargained for. The best way to determine it is to have each of your people complete for you what might very well be called a Career Guide. This consists of a series of eight questions that will tell you enough about how an individual thinks to allow you to arrive at his or her MHB. The questions follow.

1. What goals do you hope to achieve within the next three years?
2. What is the next position into which you would like to be promoted?
3. Do you feel that you are able to use all of your talents and abilities in your present sales job? (If the answer is no, please indicate which department in our company would bring out your full potential.)
4. In the course of your present duties, what do you consider most important?
5. What aspect of your present job do you enjoy most?

6. What do you like most about our company?
7. Can you make an important suggestion that would be beneficial to you and to management?
8. Are you and your family happy with your association with this company?
Why?

As you can see from the gist of these questions, a great deal can be learned about an individual's likes and dislikes. Careful scrutiny of these will, more often than not, give you that person's MHB.

An excellent exercise in planning your strategy on motivation is to list the motivational forces on a sheet of paper (with their respective definitions) and then match answers from the Career Guide with certain of the motivational forces. You might be able to narrow it down to one specific motivational force, but there will be times when two or three will be identifiable. It is at this point that you will know exactly what has to be done to motivate individuals on a *regular* basis. I hasten to add that in addition to motivating people according to their individual MHBs, it is also important to do so on a *regular* basis. Otherwise, you have what is known as the parade effect. Let me explain that one:

Picture yourself parking your automobile to do a little shopping. As you step out of your car, you hear the music of a snappy marching band as part of a parade only one block over. You don't have time to go and watch the parade, but as you walk to your immediate destination, you automatically find yourself marching in step with the music. But you are going in the opposite direction of the parade. And as you get further and further away from the music, you find that your gait is slowing down. Soon you no longer hear the music and you're right back to your usual style of walking—a lot slower than a marching step.

The motivation of people is exactly like that. It works initially, but it wears out fast. That's why field sales managers, whose people are all local, will hold a sales meeting on a weekly basis. That's why people with a tough door-to-door situation like encyclopedias and vacuum cleaners are brought in for Monday morning motivational meetings on a regular basis.

And that's why it behooves a field sales manager to find out what the MHB is of every individual on the staff and do something with it at every possible contact and as regularly as possible.

Is Enthusiasm Lacking?

You feel that you've done all that you can to motivate your sales staff, but repeatedly you say to yourself, "Enthusiasm is lacking." This may not be true of all of your people, but there are enough of them who seem to complain a lot, are not terribly excited over what is happening in their territory, and simply do not generate the enthusiasm that you would expect in anyone involved in selling. This is a definite problem found in more salespeople than we realize.

First of all, let's examine the word *enthusiasm*. What does it really mean? A good definition of *enthusiasm*, from a selling standpoint, is "a display of intense emotion born of excitement over one's endeavors." It follows, therefore, that if someone can get excited over the very idea of selling the products or services you market, then enthusiasm should be practically built-in. But how many really get excited? Consider the fact that 67 percent of salesman are, by their own admission, introverts. And you will agree that introverts don't often display much enthusiasm. So what's the answer?

The solution to this problem is really twofold. The field sales manager must first make sure that the people hired are excited about the whole idea to begin with. If that excitement doesn't come across during interviews, chances are that enthusiasm will never be generated to any great degree. So, in making selections, it behooves the manager to make certain that each individual is the excitable type who can be made even more intense emotionally.

The other aspect of the solution is applicable not only to new hirees but to existing salespeople as well. It requires that you do a certain amount of personality training at every possible opportunity. In chapter 3 we discussed sales training to a substantial degree. Let's not lose sight of the fact that personality training is definitely an integral part of sales training. We know that all people who sell do so through their own personality. The worn-out phrase, ''First you sell yourself and then you sell your product'' may sound trite, but it still holds true. And I suspect that it will hold true until the end of time. The reason is obvious. If the prospect doesn't like the sales representative at the outset of a sales interview, the chances of the sale being made are almost negligible. How do you get a prospect to like you? There's only one way: through your own personality. That's why personality training becomes a must whenever any amount of sales training is administered.

But the secondary aspect has a significant twist to it. How can a manager conduct a session on personality training through which the sales force will become more enthusiastic if the manager himself is not bubbling over with enthusiasm. And I don't mean *manufactured* enthusiasm for the purposes of the training session. I mean *genuine* enthusiasm, which is not only prevalent during the training session *but at all times*. Yes, it is imperative that a manager is enthusiastic *constantly*. It is a known fact that enthusiasm is catching. It is virtually impossible for someone to be in the presence of an enthusiastic person without some of it rubbing off. So, make a commitment now to yourself and to your future. Decide that you will be even more enthusiastic than you ever have been in the past. With that enthusiasm you will be able to promote it throughout your sales staff. If every single time that you come in contact with your people, individually or at meetings, you exude the same degree of enthusiasm that you would like to see in them, you'll soon begin to see the difference.

Motivation and enthusiasm go hand in hand. It can almost be deduced that without enthusiasm there can be no motivation. There is a human tendency always to do best that which we like to do and do well. It also follows that if we do something that we like repeatedly, we derive so much pleasure from it that enthusiasm is bound to be present in abundance. But in spite of all this we will have to admit to each other that there are individuals who simply cannot get excited and won't become enthusiastic. If one of your people falls in this category and you feel that you have done all that you possibly can to turn things around, you have a decision to make. And since you are a sales manager and one who knows well the importance of enthusiasm and motivation, that decision can only be that you must look for a replacement. One who is excitable from the very beginning and who will respond to motivation with an abundance of enthusiasm is the person you must find.

Are Quotas Hated?

At your last sales meeting you decided to try a new idea. You had heard that at many sales meetings they will conduct an after-dinner gripe session. This is the type of session where, after a hearty dinner and a few drinks, everybody lets his hair down and speaks his mind. The session went well, and you came away feeling that it was a good idea for your people to sort of vent their spleens. But as you thought about the various gripes that were voiced, you realized that almost every other one had to do with quotas. Yes, it was quite obvious that they simply hate their quotas.

Why do they hate them? For a variety of reasons. For one thing, they always are considered too high. Then there are other ramifications. They blame the home office staff for not knowing what happens on territory. So what do they know? How do they come up with such quotas? How can they be so wrong, year after year? How can they raise the quota on a product that has been sliding for several years in a row? Why should there be a quota for each product? Why can't there be one general quota for a territory and let the sales representative decide on the product mix through which to arrive at the quota?

Salespeople, it seems, will always despise those computer printouts that dictate how much dollar volume is expected on each product. In facing this problem, a sales manager must realize that there is a tremendous amount of selling to be done. Yes, the quotas have to be sold to the field staff—and every single year, if not on a monthly basis. Sold because most of selling is done through cleverly appealing to the sense of reason of the prospect. Your sales representatives are no different. When it comes to quotas, they are your prospects. They must be sold.

When your people complain about quotas, they are looking at them from their own point of view. They would rather not have these figures hanging over their heads. Some look upon quotas as mountains that are too high to climb. Others decide from the very start that they are not realistic, so why even try? Still others decide that they don't mean anything anyway. They feel that they are tools of management through which to prod the sales force into bringing in more sales. Whatever the reason, it is always born from individual attitudes.

Now, we all know that changing attitudes is difficult. People are always apt to build a stone wall around their pet ideas. To get through to them is not always simple. But prospects are hardheaded too. They build walls around themselves and their ideas, and we expect our people to get through. So why give up on this matter?

The way to sell quotas is to reason with your people, particularly prior to handing out quotas at the annual sales meeting. (Incidentally, that's always the best way to do it if it is at all possible. Sending the quotas in the mail is not always the best way to present them to your staff. If it has to be done that way, then the covering letter should do a great deal of selling along the lines we are about to discuss.) Yes, you reason with them by turning the tables and asking them to put themselves in the shoes of the staff people at the home office. You explain that a company cannot be operated without a budget. The budget establishes where the money will be spent in accordance with the sales that will be brought in. How about the money that will be spent in manufacturing? How much of each product is to be manufactured? How much will it cost? It becomes crystal clear, you explain, that figures must be developed upon which to base these expenditures, especially for manufacturing. A plan must come about. This plan must be companywide. It will involve everybody, including each individual in your particular area. So a quota is not really a prodding device, it is a plan. A plan of action. A plan designed to keep the company profitable. And if the company remains profitable, everyone's job is secure.

Now, you continue to explain, people don't necessarily get fired because they didn't attain the quota of a sliding product. No doubt some consideration is given to that fact when an evaluation of the individual is being done. But in cold, hard facts, this does not become a totally disqualifying factor when it comes to raises, promotions, etc.

So far you have appealed to their good sense of organization, planning, profit. So now you shift gears. Now you appeal to their egos. You explain that people who sell are always known as leaders. They are not ever followers. They are leaders because they go out in the field and create sales where ordinarily there may not have been any. That's leadership in its finest sense. And if they are leaders, they have a purpose. A purpose is a goal. A goal is a quota. Without a quota, sales representatives would be flying blind. Making as many sales as possible—what does that mean from the standpoint of a goal? After all, we all know that goal setting is something that all successful leaders take part in. So, what's the big fuss? The only difference, you explain, is that they probably don't like the fact that such goals are set for them by people in staff positions at the home office: the market researchers, the administrative assistants.

Here is a good exercise to counteract such feelings: Prior to distributing the quota printouts and right after you have done all of this effective selling, tell everyone that for the next few minutes they are going to play the part of management. Tell everyone that they are going to list all of their products and assign a quota for each product for the ensuing year. Then give them enough time to think about it and do it fairly systematically. You know exactly what's going to happen. No one is going to develop quotas that are equal to or below existing sales. Every single individual will push up figures substantially for the coming year. (If they don't know what existing sales are, you certainly have learned something, haven't you?) When this exercise has been completed, pass out the printouts. Give everyone a chance to make the interesting comparison and then ask how many feel that the quotas are very close to their own individual, personal projections. In most cases you will find that people are happy to volunteer that they had set quotas for themselves that were equal to or higher than those handed down by the home office.

Obviously, this is only one way to solve the quota problem. You can come up with many others. All of them, of course, will fall into the basic categories of reasoning and appealing to the ego of sales representatives. Some managers seem to run away from the problem on a regular basis. When it comes up during a field visit, they give it only lip service and change the subject. That's really the wrong thing to do. It is much better to discuss the subject rationally and change attitudes whenever possible. It is wise, for instance, to take advantage of opportunities for selling quotas whenever they present themselves. For instance, when Mary Smith ends up selling 125 percent of quota on a particular product, you can and should remind her that the quota that she thought so high was far from high after all. It sounds like an ''I told you so'' technique, but it doesn't have that type of effect. Mary is so happy that you are mentioning the 125 percent that she won't mind your reminding her that she complained about that particular quota when it was first given to her. Naturally, you also commend her during the same conversation, but the point is made. Do this with a number of your people and you will find that complaints about quotas will diminish substantially.

The same type of technique can be employed when writing a memorandum. Let's say you are thanking one of your sales representatives, by memo, for following up on a product complaint at your request. At the end of the memorandum you would say something like, ''P.S. Delighted to note that you are well over quota on just about every product in the line. I knew you could do it, John, that's why I didn't take your complaints about your quota seriously. A good sales rep always comes out on top.''

Of course, a sales manager can always make certain that quotas don't become monstrosities for his or her people. The way to do this is to stay right on top of them on a monthly basis. It's very easy to look at a one-year projection of quotas, notice the quarterly totals, and then check the sales figures of your people at the end of each quarter to see how closely they are coming to their quotas. This makes a lot of sense, but it's not good enough. When an individual is lagging behind badly after two months of a quarter, it often becomes impossible to make up for lost time in the four weeks that remain. What's worse, many of your people who would be confronted with such a circumstance will most likely throw up their hands in disgust, deciding that it's too late to make up for that lost time, so why worry about it. A good sales manager stays current with quotas on a *monthly* basis. You must know at the end of every single month exactly where every one of your people stands on every product in the line. Certainly this is not hard to determine. You have monthly sales figures provided to you by the home office and you have a yearly quota for every one of your people broken down by month. A brief phone call to alert an individual to a quota problem saves a lot of grief at the end of the quarter. Furthermore, it is another reason for you to make contact. Remember? The more contact the better. Obviously, you don't call with the attitude that you're going to attack. You are calling because you are "surprised" at the sales that are below quota, and you want to know how you may help. With that approach, how can anybody resent the contact you are making?

In field sales management, one truism seems to come up over and over again. The people who complain to the hilt about quotas are usually the people who are at the bottom of the pile. It is very rare when the productive and successful members of your staff make derogatory remarks about a quota. They take it in stride, dig in, stay positive, and bring home the bacon.

One last word about quotas. If your company has a profit-sharing program, don't fail to capitalize on a golden opportunity. Refer the complainer to the profit-sharing plan. Explain that quotas bring in profits. Profits go into a number of places, one of which is the profit-sharing plan. "So, what's the problem? Bring in more sales and thereby more profit and you will put many more dollars in your pocket."

Are Sales Contests Boring?

Your company is most likely one that believes in sales contests, and more often than not there is one being held. However, even though you talk it up as often as is possible, you find that your people don't get excited enough over the contests or the prizes involved.

This is a very generalized problem. There was a time when any kind of contest would get people excited. There was a time when stamps or points would make people work hard to get them. A coffee table, a camera, a black-and-white TV set, or a set of golf clubs were stimulants to most people. But no longer. Because of the affluent society in America today, items of this nature are no longer craved. Most people have them. So why get excited about a contest that will "give me items I already have?"

Most companies have come to realize that a sales contest must have grandiose prizes in order to excite a sales staff. In fact, most contests will now offer expensive and exotic cruises for the winner and the spouse or two-week vacations in far-away places or very substantial gifts like a new automobile or a boat. And yet, the amount of excitement that you would expect to be generated just isn't there.

Well, first of all, most national sales contests that originate from the home office are held over a substantial span of time. Some cover a ninety-day selling period, but most of them, especially when the prizes are very large in scope, will extend over a period of six months. Now, salespeople are usually "today" people. At best, they are "this week" people. They simply are not the type of people who think six months ahead. Most of them think three months from now is almost an eternity. As a result, the announcement of a contest that will end six months from now is looked upon as "something I'll look into later on." It just doesn't have any immediate impact. Even if the first prize is awesome, the impact is not felt immediately. So, they just don't get excited about it. This is a very human phenomenon. That's why most people don't start to worry about income taxes until it's almost time to file a return.

The field sales manager, therefore, has to overcome this problem by doing two things. First, it is important that the national contest be segmented to the local region, district, or whatever. You do this by sending out bulletins that bring out significant facts. For instance, in one bulletin you would point out that "in our area we have a group of salespeople who represent 15 percent of the national sales force. That means that we have a 15 percent chance of winning these prizes at the outset. The next question is, Who in our group will win the first, second, or third prize?" Statements of this nature make your people realize that these prizes are quite attainable. And that's why attention should be given to the contest rather than sloughing it off.

The second thing you do is even more significant. Every month (twice a month if that is at all possible) you publish a standing of your people in relation to the rest of the sales force in the country. Now, when they receive these standings, they will be looking at where they stand nationally, but more importantly they will be noticing how they stand in the district. After all, nobody wants to be at the bottom of the totem pole. You can see, therefore, that by regionalizing a national contest in this way, the chances of your people becoming more excited are substantially increased.

And, of course, to involve the spouse is a wise idea. When sending bulletins of this nature to the homes of your salespeople, make sure they are addressed to the couple rather than the individual. This, obviously, increases the chances for the development of excitement, because if the contest appeals to the spouse even more than to the sales person, you now have a partner on your side.

Then, as far as contests are concerned, a field sales manager should always have localized contests going on as often as possible. These contests should never run more than a month and should be germane to the area. For instance, if there is a very plush and not very affordable restaurant in the general area, two dinners could mean something. If there is an unusual sporting event for which tickets are extremely hard to get and are probably very expensive, then two tickets for this event mean something. A getaway weekend for a couple in a suite in the finest hotel in the area is always considered of value. But, I repeat, these should always be on a monthly basis. Even if you don't have a contest every single month, when you do, don't have it run beyond thirty days. You'll discover that a great deal of excitement can be stimulated by using the local and the short-range approach.

Then, in most areas of the United States there is an excellent, tailor-made contest right at your doorstep. In most cities there is a chapter of Sales and Marketing Executives International. This is a worldwide organization offering excellent programs. One of their yearly programs is the awarding of the Distinguished Salesperson's Award. If you are a member of the organization, and you should be, your company can participate at the local level. You simply conduct a contest involving your people, or you nominate the individual who has the best sales record. That person is then honored at the banquet held by the organization, where trophies are presented to all winners of the Distinguished Salesperson's Award. On the occasion of that particular banquet, you take one or more tables to accommodate all of your people and their spouses, and when the winners of these awards are called, your specific individual will go to the stage, be photographed with the other winners from other companies, all holding their trophies, will see that picture in the newspaper, will be congratulated by those in attendance, etc. This is always a gala event, with an important guest speaker, and it is usually the most important function in the club year.

When it's all said and done, however, how you yourself react to contests will also determine how much excitement your people will muster. If you act enthusiastically about a contest—as though you have a chance of winning the prize yourself—this enthusiasm will spill over. It is contagious. And enthusiasm always creates excitement. It becomes important, therefore, that you always study the details of a contest and be able to answer any questions that may come up. Besides, complete knowledge of a contest on your part shows that you are very interested in it. And like everything else, when you know your subject matter well, you can act very enthusiastic about it. So, when it's all said and done, people don't get excited about sales contests because those who run them are not entirely cognizant of what must be done to create the excitement.

While you may not have complete control over what the home office is doing, you certainly can apply the principles described here to make your people much more interested in sales contests. And this is important. Because the more interested you can make them, the more sales will be brought about. And that's a great part of your job, isn't it?

Is Competitive Spirit Lacking?

Remember when, in January, you were chatting with Jack Robinson and you said, "Jack, I'm sure you're proud of finishing up this past year as the top man in the district, and I'm equally certain that you plan on not relinquishing that honor this year." And Jack said, "Oh, I don't know, maybe I ought to give someone else a chance this year."

You were shocked, stunned, mystified. You couldn't believe what you heard. You really didn't know what to say. You simply didn't understand how the top person in your district could lack competitive spirit. You took your thoughts one step further. If the top person has no competitive spirit, how about the rest of the people? They didn't come out on top. Maybe the reason that they didn't is because they weren't competitive enough. Something seems to be wrong.

There certainly is, and it's something that should concern you greatly. If a strong competitive spirit is lacking in your organization, the sales figures that won Jack Robinson the top spot are most likely much lower than what they could have been. That's enough to give you several nights of no sleep, but it's true.

Look at it this way. Why does the underdog in an

athletic contest many times win against almost impossible odds? Why does the home field advantage so many times go down the drain during an important football game? Why does a professional golfer who is four strokes behind in a tournament with only six holes to go emerge as the winner? The answer, more often than not, is that a very high competitive spirit makes it all possible.

Selling is no different. There must be a high competitive spirit among every individual in your organization in order for you to reap the most sales out of your area. Not only must there be much competition among the salespeople themselves, but, as a group, they must be very competitive with other districts throughout the country. But the question that usually comes up is, Aren't most people competitive because they were born that way? Aren't they competitive because it's in their blood? Aren't they competitive because they were brought up that way? Not necessarily. Obviously, all of these factors help, but it is still very possible to bring out a highly competitive spirit in people who ordinarily would not feel that way. And to do this is not at all difficult.

Earlier in this chapter we talked about the various motivational forces to which people respond. One of these was recognition. We said that people who respond to this motivational force are those who thrive on praise and publicity. Well, let's take it one step further. They also thrive on being recognized as the winner in any given competition. You say, "But we already talked about that. We already went over sales contests, their prizes, etc." That's true, but a lot more can be done. For instance, a good sales manager finds all sorts of reasons to award plaques, trophies, pins, etc. They really are not that expensive. In fact, for the results produced they are very inexpensive. (I never ceased to be amazed at how inexpensive certain trophies are, large trophies, the ones with the marble or highly polished wooden bases and that have two or three tiers making them some two or three feet high.) But I am never amazed at the look on the face of the recipient when such trophies are presented. Nor am I amazed to enter the den or playroom or sometimes even the living room of an individual to find a host of trophies standing on the mantel over the fireplace or on a specific shelf that lends itself to the greatest visibility upon entrance to the room. Why? It's obvious. People are so delighted to obtain this type of recognition that they want everyone else to know about it.

I shall never forget a conversation I once had with a salesman. He was to appear at graduation ceremonies at the conclusion of a sales course. He told me that he couldn't make it. I expressed surprise. I said, "You mean you're going to miss the opportunity to accept a diploma in front of sixty-five people and also miss out on having your picture in the newspaper?" You'll never believe what his answer was. He said, "Well, I belong to a bowling league, and on the same night we will be bowling for the last time this season. I'm so close to that huge trophy I can taste it. I wouldn't miss it for the world." You see, the diploma was important, but the trophy was much bigger and much more exciting.

Find as many ways as you possibly can to make awards that promote recognition and greatly increase a competitive spirit. First develop the categories and then decide what the awards will be. For instance, here are some of the categories that many sales managers use:

Largest order taken this month
Largest order taken this year
Most new accounts opened this month

Most new accounts opened this year
Most calls made this month
Most calls made this year
Best ratio of calls to orders this month
Best ratio of calls to orders this year
Most competitive information obtained
Most dealer meetings held

You see, the categories are not hard to develop. Depending upon your type of operation and the type of statistical records that you keep, you can not only use the above categories but add many more to them. The more awards, the better.

Now, let's talk about the types of awards. Develop one source for all of your awards. A trophy shop will be able to supply you with almost any type of award that you may be interested in. By getting them all from one source you can establish quantity prices, discounts. Then pick out items like plaques, trophies, pins, desk sets, Paul Revere bowls, silver trays; the list is endless. But *always* have the person's name on the trophy. Remember, a trophy without the winner's name on it is almost worthless. If the cost of also engraving what the trophy is for is prohibitive, it's perfectly okay to leave that part out. The recipient can always discuss it with anyone who asks, glowing with pride in the process. But the name *must never* be left out.

Naturally, the awards made for monthly achievements are always smaller than the ones for yearly achievements. But the larger they are, the better. As far as pins are concerned, you should check with your home office before you have a specially designed pin made up locally. Usually the home office can give you a variation of the five-year, ten-year, etc., pins where the mold has already been made.

The presentation of these awards is almost as important

as the awards themselves. Never mail an award to a recipient or make an individual presentation when you are both alone. Awards should always be made when all the others are present. So the ideal place is at your sales meetings. If you hold a few sales meetings a year, then that's the place to do it. Even if there are only one or two sales meetings a year, let all of these awards accumulate, but that's when you present them. Because that's how you develop the spirit of competition. Whenever someone is beaten out for an award by a very small margin, or even a large one, there is always that feeling that it will not happen again. That feeling that the person must try harder. That's what competition is all about.

You might argue that holding the presentation for a sales meeting might be a long time to wait. Yes, that's true. But you do something in the meantime. You announce to all of your people, via a memorandum or a sales bulletin, that trophies, plaques, or whatever have been won by the following people for the following reasons. You continue to do this as each award is won. You get a great deal of mileage through this type of correspondence. You also congratulate individuals as you contact them for other reasons and discuss the type of award that has been won and explain that it will be presented at the next sales meeting.

It has been said that in many ways most of us are kids who have never grown up. This statement couldn't be truer when it comes to the development of a competitive spirit and certainly the winning of prizes. And it all revolves around recognition. There isn't a single human being that doesn't respond to recognition. Oh, they may say that they don't. They may pooh-pooh the whole idea sometimes. They try to act blase, but deep inside they like being recognized. And they'll fight to get that recognition. That special prize always brings about the competitive spirit.

There is many a branch office throughout this country out of which operates the local sales staff. It is not uncommon to see in the waiting rooms of these branch offices the trophies that have been won by the district or the division. They're always highly polished and in a glass-enclosed cabinet. It is obvious just how proud the people behind those trophies are. But many of them go even further. In the very same waiting room, and on a very visible wall, will be the pictures of the top three salespeople. And these pictures are generally changed monthly or quarterly. Or they'll have a huge plaque where the names of the leading salespeople are entered as they achieve certain heights. I can assure you that all of the money and effort that goes into such waiting-room displays is well worth it. I have been told by many sales representatives how proud they feel when they enter the branch office and see their picture on the wall or their name on plaques and trophies.

Now, some sales managers are well aware of what we've been discussing but will then go a bit too far. They think that they can develop a competitive spirit by motivating people through fear or by "bringing up the rear" awards. Well, fear is the worst motivator in existence. It just doesn't work. If you continue to remind an individual what the horrible consequences are if a particular goal is not achieved, that individual, upon realizing that the goal cannot be achieved, will develop a very poor attitude. More importantly, that individual will look for a job where fear need not be contended with. A sales manager must never resort to threats in an effort to motivate people or to develop a competitive spirit. It's the wrong approach.

The same negative result is obtained with "bringing up the rear" awards. No one likes to be given the booby prize. No one likes to walk to the stage or the head table to receive a prize for being the worst. I realize that most of the time it is done in jest and that there is applause and many smiles. But inwardly the individual is bleeding. What have you done in the way of motivation? Nothing. In fact, you may have broken the individual's spirit in the process, not to mention the embarrassment experienced. Some of these awards are downright ridiculous anyway. I've seen people awarded a hard-boiled egg, a child's rattler, a cut-up golf ball, a tennis racket with no strings, a burnt-out lightbulb, an infant's pacifier. Sure, there's always laughter when such awards are made, but at whose expense? And I often wonder how this is at all possible in the sales profession. We keep telling each other constantly that we must think positively. We must not allow negative thoughts to enter our minds. We must always accentuate the positive and eliminate the negative. Well, what could be more negative than to award a prize for failure? No matter how ridiculous the prize may be.

Let us not forget the real meaning of motivation. If a sales manager is to motivate his people, then he might "provide a motive." This calls for much thought, planning, and above all, a great deal of common sense. But every minute spent on this aspect of sales management is extremely worthwhile. To insure success, a knowledgeable field sales manager makes certain that the entire group supervised is always highly motivated. The opposite is disastrous.

Please note that this chapter on motivation at best

barely scratches the surface of a very complex subject. Much has been published on it, and I strongly recommend that you read as much of the available material as possible. As you do, not only will you be impressed at how much research has been done on motivation, but you'll also realize how directly related it is to the performance of people who sell.

6
Expenses and Expense Reports

At least one of your salespeople continues to submit an expense report on a regular basis that you always feel is not correct. You feel like questioning some of the items but you refrain from doing so because you don't want to be picayune. Yet, in your own heart, you have every reason to believe that some of the items are trumped up or that some of them have been vastly exaggerated. You know this is a problem and you want to do something about it and you wonder what can be done.

Do You Have a "Gyp-Sheet" Artist on Staff?

For some unknown reason, the expense account has always been regarded by many salespeople as another source of income. Why this misconception no one will ever figure out. I say misconception because an expense check was merely designed to reimburse an individual for *legitimate* expenses incurred while in the process of making sales calls. However, tell an individual that there is an "unlimited" expense account associated with a position and the eyebrows are immediately raised. Why? Because the possibility of using the expense account as another source of income immediately flashes through the person's mind.

The thrill is not always in the additional cash realized as much as in the fact that the individual has been successful in strategically maneuvering the acceptance of an expenditure that was not actually made or authorized. There is a classic story that, though humorous, proves this point conclusively.

There was once a salesman who was transferred from the South to the New England area. Every eight weeks he was scheduled to make a swing of northern Maine and cover the existing accounts as well as opening new ones. His first coverage in this area was in late October, and he ran into a tremendous snowstorm, something he hardly expected. Determined not to let this stop him, he went to a shoe store, bought a pair of hip boots, and proceeded to trudge through the snow drifts to cover the assigned territory. On his expense report at the end of the week he had a miscellaneous item of sixteen dollars with an asterisk. The explanation at the bottom of the report stated, "I ran into an unexpected snowstorm in Maine and had to buy a pair of hip boots for sixteen dollars in order to cover my accounts." His sales manager crossed out the sixteen-dollar item and readjusted the total. He explained on the report that the salesman should have been prepared for all eventualities, and this expenditure was not permissible.

But the salesman was one who didn't give up too easily. On the following week's report he entered the item again.

This time he went into a lengthier explanation. "You will notice from my call report that I did a substantial amount of business even in the middle of a snowstorm. The orders I wrote more than justify the expenditure of sixteen dollars. Please approve this item." But the sales manager was just as obstinate. He disallowed it a second time and explained, "Items of clothing are not to be entered in your expense account."

At the end of the third week the salesman submitted a very normal expense report. There were no deviations, nothing that would seem in any way abnormal. But at the very bottom he entered an intriguing notation, "The boots are in here. You find them."

One effective way to handle problems of this nature is to make sure that the rules are spelled out at the very beginning. Even before a new salesperson is allowed to go on territory, you should thoroughly explain the purpose of an expense account and how important it is never to abuse the privilege. If your company does not supply the sales staff with a complete list of which items are permissible and which are not, then the responsibility of doing just that falls on your own shoulders. Make out such a list, as completely as you can, taking all possibilities into consideration, and give the list to the new salesperson as a guide. Then you avoid the general excuse of, "I didn't know that such an item could not be expensed."

Still another avenue of attacking the problem is to make sure that you never bend over backward and allow something that is not allowable just because a salesperson is new on the job or because you're dealing with the biggest producer in your district. If you rationalize because of newness, your leadership is wanting. If high production influences you, a huge monster is in the making. As ridiculous and unfair as it may sound, there seems to be an unwritten rule that the better the sales representative, the more lenient superiors are with the expense account. And when you get into this sort of a rut, it is much like bribery. The demands get bigger and not in proportion with the returns. Let a situation of this nature get out of hand and the ability of management to regain control is greatly hampered.

Like the old story about the salesman who was the very best in the company, always brought in the biggest sales, won all of the contests, was extremely loyal to the company, but always took undue advantage of his expense account. There were times that the items he included and the size of them were far from tolerable. The district sales manager was really at fault. As long as he continued to approve the expense reports, this greedy individual was paid regularly. But one day the national sales manager decided he had had enough. He had given repeated warnings to the district sales manager, who had mildly transmitted them to the salesman. None of them, however, had ever produced any change in the situation. So one day the national sales manager told the district manager, who was visiting the home office, that obviously the time had come to take matters into his own hands. He said, "I want you to know that I am writing to Bill Smith directly and giving him his last warning." This he did with the following note:

Dear Bill:

You have been taking advantage of your expense account for over a year and a half. You have been repeatedly warned by your district sales manager and have not heeded these warnings.

Unless you immediately stop this practice, you will leave me no alternative than to terminate your employment with the company.
> Cordially,
> Jack Hamilton
> National Sales Manager

By return mail, Hamilton received his own letter with the following notation on it:

Dear Jack,
Look what some son of a bitch wrote me and signed your name to it.
> Regards,
> Bill

Yes, that's how far it can go. It can get to the point where control is lost completely. But when this happens, a sales manager has allowed it to happen. It's a perfect example of the well-known adage, "You give them an inch and they take a mile."

Is the "Open" Expense Account a Failure?

One of your better sales representatives submits an expense report that, unlike the previous ones, contains a host of nonpermissible items. You discuss it with him in a very gentle manner, and he listens to all you have to say. But the retort is a common one. He looks at you and says, "But I thought I was on an open expense account."

The problem here is that the word *open* was never *really* defined to the individual. Some companies place all of their salespeople on what is known as a fixed expense. This means that each territory, having been completely researched, has been assigned a specific figure to cover all possible expenses on any given month. Under these circumstances, the person covering that territory is regularly paid that fixed amount every month without having to submit a detailed expense report. This arrangement has its disadvantages as well as its advantages. There is no question that it helps the home office from a budgetary standpoint, expenses are foreseen as much as a year in advance without variations, and it also keeps a tightly sealed lid on each territory. But the sales staff looks at it from another angle. They are quick to realize that if they reduce the amount of travel or coverage and never take anyone to lunch, there is money to be made on such an arrangement.

So the better arrangement is to have an open expense account, with the word *open* meaning more that it is capable of handling whatever is spent rather than that it's open to handle indiscriminate and unjustifiable expenditures. It's a delicate situation, to be sure. You cannot set dollar limits on any particular type of spending because, if you do, you will find that your people will spend up to that specific dollar limit. So the best solution is to tell the members of your staff that although they are on open expense, each of their expense reports will be carefully scrutinized by you before you approve them. And then do it. Don't just warn people without ever following through. In fact, it is excellent strategy to every so often ask an individual to justify an expenditure for which there is not a receipt. For instance, tips might seem to be a little high, even though there was hoteling involved. If the length of the stay was relatively short, like a day or two, chances are that there wasn't that much luggage to be carried. Under those circumstances, tips could be scrutinized by you, and, although they are eventually approved, the individual would know that you are carefully checking all entries in the submitted expense report.

Is "Entertainment" a Problem?

There are some salespeople who keep entertainment within their territories at an absolute minimum. Then there are those who seem dedicated to the theory that they must do a substantial amount of entertaining in order to get people to do business with them. With those in the latter category, a very strict attitude must be taken. They are usually the type who get customers in an entertainment habit. By this I mean that once they start this business of taking the customer out to lunch each time they come into the area, then the customer expects just that.

Naturally, taking someone out to lunch or dinner has its place in selling, particularly when the prospect or the customer is a volume buyer. But this does not have to come about in connection with every single sales call or every time the salesperson is in the general area. One way to break a prospect or customer from the habit is to call on the account either early in the morning or midafternoon, well away from the time of day when eating would be in order. In any event, the "entertainment" aspect of selling should not be reduced to a favor in return for an order. It should be used as a tool for getting a new account or for maintaining an old one by cementing relations on an occasional basis. Unless this practice is kept in check, the amount of expense money that could be utilized would far exceed the return on the investment. There have been cases where a salesman has taken a prospect out six, eight, even ten times in search of an order. And when the order did come through, it wasn't even enough to pay for the meals.

However, even in instances where entertainment is not only indicated but more than justified, it can be kept down to a reasonable level. For instance, lunch, in almost any restaurant, is less expensive than dinner. And many times for the exact same dish. So, wherever possible, it is much more economical to entertain someone at lunch than it is at dinner. Furthermore, it's not necessary to bring a prospect or customer to the most exclusive restaurant in the area. It may be prestigious but it is also terribly expensive. In fact, it could work against you. You should remind your salespeople that entertaining at the most expensive restaurant might impress some but it might turn off others. It would certainly not sit well with someone who was on the edge of doing business with you but thinks your price is a little high. That someone might well decide that the reason your price is "a little high" is because you spend altogether too much money entertaining people lavishly—and why should he pay for that? Above all, you must impress upon your sales staff that there are far too many freeloaders in any industry. It is so important to recognize a freeloader and know how to deal with him or her that I suggest that you cover this thoroughly at one of your sales meetings, and to make it easy for you, the following presentation, all prepared for you, will make the point quite well and very effectively:

Regardless of what territory you cover, there will always be a substantial number of prospects who are very happy to have you take them out to lunch or dinner. In fact, they never turn down an invitation, even if they don't have any business for you. Some will accept your generosity knowing full well that giving you an order is something that will never come about. Turning down the offer of free drinks and a free meal would be a departure from their normal character. They are usually known as freeloaders. They are always too busy to see you during business hours, but if you suggest lunch or dinner, they leap at the opportunity.

First of all, you must learn to recognize a freeloader when you become involved with one. Not only will he accept *every* invitation that you extend, but he will go so far as to invite himself to have lunch with you at your expense. Furthermore, you'll find that he will casually inquire as to where you are taking him, just to make sure that it is a restaurant where liquor is served. To the average freeloader the drinks are more important than the food.

Second, you must become an expert at evaluating the progress you are making, business-wise, with each person who puts a dent in your expense account. After two bouts at a restaurant something of value should develop for you. Especially since the *second* meal will have been your *third* meeting. You see, between meals you strategically work in an abstinence interview by calling on him in the midmorning or midafternoon within two weeks of the previous meal. (His conscience will cause him to see you, even though he may be busy.) If the account is big enough and the potential impressive, three meals (representing five interviews) is as far as you need go with anyone without becoming a benefactor. And naturally you must always ask for the order on every occasion including an eating spree with drinks. Breaking bread together is a warm and pleasant way to socialize, but don't lose sight of your mission. You are not a goodwill ambassador. Nor are you one who is testing different restaurants to see how good the food is. You are there to sell something, and you won't sell without asking for the order.

Is Evaluation of Expense Reports Too Time-Consuming?

You supervise sixteen people in your district, and every cotton-picking week you receive sixteen expense reports that you must approve. Naturally your conscience always tells you never to approve them routinely. You must look at them carefully and determine if they are in order and if all expenditures are justified. You consider this a really time-consuming bore. You wonder how important it is to spend all this time on this menial task. Yet, you know that you can't put it off because unless you approve these reports, your people won't get paid. So, there are times when you rush through them as quickly as you can, but you still say to yourself, "This is the most boring aspect of my job."

Well, it doesn't have to be. There are two reasons why you can make the approval of expense reports a little more interesting. One, because you consider them a management tool—which they are. There's a lot to be learned from them. Secondly, you can develop substantial statistical data from them that makes it easier to go through them each week. For instance, as a management tool, you can evaluate your salespeople from the standpoint of neatness, correctness, deviations, greediness, adherence to itinerary, lavish entertainment, and repeated entertainment of unproductive prospects or customers. I repeat, there is much to be learned if one merely looks for some of these things every single time that an expense report is being approved.

On the other side of the coin is the statistical information that can be derived. This is done by taking large ledger-type sheets, assigning one to each of your salespeople. Then every time you are approving an expense report, you transfer total figures from the expense report to columns on the ledger sheet under the headings of car expense, entertainment, tips, hoteling, meals, tolls, etc. Virtually all of the headings from the totals of the expense report become headings on your ledger sheet. Then, at a glance, you can take totals, perhaps quarterly, and you are able to compare totals from one territory to another to see if the variances are substantial or justified. Statistics of this nature become extremely helpful when you begin to suspect an individual of taking advantage of the expense account. Also, these statistics become very valuable when planning budgets for the ensuing year or when splitting territories or when you are about to hold a performance evaluation counseling session with an individual in your employ.

However, under no circumstances, should you ever delegate this responsibility to a secretary or anyone else who might be doing some paperwork for you. The whole idea of the exercise, in addition to bringing you more in tune with what is being spent by whom, is to bring these figures to your attention personally. Because it's when a particular figure seems out of line that you will be able to take the appropriate action. If this kind of scrutiny is done by others, deviations will slip through without any attention.

Are Falsifications Hard to Prove?

You have one or two salespeople in your district or division whose expense reports are not that far out of line, but you suspect some falsification. You wish that you could prove it.

You can. It's not as hard as some people think. It's just a case of playing detective once in a while without upsetting the apple cart. You never want to play detective and give a prospect or customer the idea that you are checking on your people. Many of them would resent such an operation. They would wonder about you, your company, and even the sales representative who calls on them. So this is not a very good idea. On the other hand, there are many things you can do to make it difficult for your people to falsify expense reports.

One way is to *insist upon* receipts. Yes, receipts for almost every conceivable thing. You may think this is silly. And so do many salespeople. They will think it quite embarrassing to ask for a receipt for a bridge toll when it represents an expenditure of only fifteen cents. But that's not the idea. The idea is to insist upon receipts on everything, no matter how small the amount. It's a case of getting people accustomed to *always* asking for receipts. Besides, such receipts serve an additional purpose. When Joe Jones claims that he went to Treasure Island, it's a very comforting thing to see the receipt from the bridge you must cross to get there. It's just another way of keeping people honest and in line with their itineraries.

Now let's get back to playing detective. Of course it's unpleasant. You could argue from here till doomsday that this is not your job. Your job is sales management, not playing detective. No question. But unfortunately some of it is necessary every so often. How do you do it? It's easy. You find a good excuse, as legitimate as possible, to call a prospect or a customer who, say, was recently entertained according to an expense report. And you broach the subject casually. For instance, I can easily recall how I handled it in the pharmaceutical industry. Here is one example:

A physician was performing a clinical study on one of our drugs. The home office was in regular contact, sending him sample materials to use on his patients, forms to be filled out to substantiate the clinical study, etc. I was a district manager and was kept fully informed of what was going on. So was the salesman who covered the territory in which the doctor practiced. The home office required interim reports during the study. Dates were set from the very start as to when these reports would be submitted. Doctors, of course, get very busy and slip up on meeting these deadlines. It would usually require follow-up by either the district manager or the representative who called on the doctor.

One day I received a notice from the home office that a particular doctor was two weeks behind in his interim report on a clinical study. I noticed that the detail man had been sent a copy of this notice. I checked and found that on the previous week my man had had lunch with this particular doctor. It was clearly noted in his daily call report and on his expense report. I seized this golden opportunity.

I phoned the physician, identified myself, and then said, "I'm terribly sorry to disturb you, Doctor, especially since what I'm about to discuss with you could have been covered by my man when he had lunch with you only last week." I paused momentarily, and he jumped into the conversation. He said, "Hold it. I didn't have lunch with your man last week. In fact, I haven't seen your man for quite a few weeks, maybe even months. In fact, I can't remember the last time I saw him."

I expressed surprise, naturally, and quickly recovered by saying that perhaps I had made a mistake from my reports. In any event, I proceeded quietly to request him to submit his interim report. Well, this was most significant. I checked more deeply and discovered that my man had shown a previous luncheon only three weeks prior with the same doctor and in the last two months had shown four different calls on this doctor by virtue of the fact that close contact was necessary because of the clinical study going on. That evening I phoned my man at the motel in which he was staying and told him of this revolting development. He had no recourse. He was practically speechless. I offered no immediate solution. I told him that on Saturday morning, upon return from his trip, I would like to meet with him at 10:00 A.M. for a counseling session. When we met, I read him the riot act. I explained to him that there was absolutely no reason for such falsifications and that had he not been with the company for over two years, it would have meant immediate dismissal. So, I gave him one more chance, with the understanding that *never* would I ever tolerate falsification of any reports under any circumstances.

Naturally, it's not easy to nail down every single falsification. But it's amazing how many of them can be brought to the surface by thinking in the right direction as a manager. It's simply a case of constantly bearing in mind that outside salespeople know that supervision is not that complete. That it's really impossible to be terribly complete, Their thinking goes something like, "Oh, they'll never find out."

I hasten to add that the particular salesman in the story I just related never again falsified a report. Periodic checks proved this.

7
Recruiting

Remember how disappointed you were the last time you ran an ad for a salesperson and you only received eight replies? What's worse, not one of them was qualified. Most likely, you wondered why. *Why* would so few salespeople answer your ad?

Do Your Newspaper Ads Pull?

Well, there are reasons for everything—even for why people don't answer specific ads. For one thing, are you sure you ran it in the right newspaper? There are many good-sized cities with two or three major newspapers in them. Invariably, however, one of them carries the lion's share of classified advertising. Check with an advertising agency to determine which is the proper newspaper to use. In fact, let the agency place it for you. It costs you no more, and you get expert advice along with the service. Ads placed in that newspaper *always* pull. When people are looking for a job, they buy *that* paper. Ads placed in the other newspapers in that town are not only a waste of money but could work against you. Some people will rationalize that you must be desperate and don't keep your salespeople if you're advertising in a newspaper not used by most people. So, the first rule in newspaper advertising has to be, Make sure your ad is running in the right paper for that area.

Then there's the question of signature. Think about your ad that failed. Did you make sure that the ad contained your firm's name and the name of the title of the executive doing the recruiting? "Elementary," you say. Yet, over 50 percent of sales-recruiting ads are still "blind," despite the fact that most salespeople won't write to a box number. Many won't even reply to the personnel department. They only answer ads when they know the name of the company and the name of the executive in the sales department. They want no surprises, and certainly they don't want to be caught replying to a blind ad run by their present employer.

Then there's the problem of position. Do you remember exactly where the ad was run? Was it simply under "Help Wanted"? That, incidentally, is a dreadful mistake. The ad may well get buried among dishwashers, carpenters, hostesses, and most people just can't be bothered to read every single ad. Just about every newspaper uses the heading "Sales Help Wanted." That's where it belongs in order to get the most visibility by the most qualified people. And the smarter salespeople, the ones you want to attract, go directly to that heading.

Here are some other checkpoints you may want to consider in solving the problem of poor pickings from newspaper ads:

- Did you run a border around your ad to make it stand out against the others?
- Did you include a phone number to catch those who want to do something about it immediately? (Incidentally, don't make the typical mistake of the average field sales manager who places an ad in the Sunday newspaper and leaves on Monday morning for a week's field trip. You have to be around to handle the calls and to do some on-the-spot screening in the process, which saves lots of interviewing time.)
- Did you tell it like it really is? It's a big mistake to say that "Our sales representatives earn $20,000 per year" if this is only true of one of your people while the other forty-nine are in the $12–15,000 bracket. Such deviousness may fill territories quickly, but it also increases turnover, and that's costly. Besides, credibility in an ad is a must. The sharper salespeople can quickly see through the exaggerated claims and won't bother with the ad. Either give the *average* yearly income of your sales staff or leave the earnings out completely.
- Did you run a trite headline? We are all familiar with the one that reads, "We only hire future sales managers." Believe it or not, there *are* some people who don't ever want to be sales managers; they simply don't want the responsibility. More importantly, they may have been promised the world in their last position, are now disenchanted, and don't want to start off with a new company that makes promises even before an interview.

Do Employment Services Produce?

Recently you received a telephone call from a local employment agency offering to help you with your recruiting needs, and you turned them down. You stated flatly, "We have never obtained good applicants from employment agencies, so we have now decided not to use them at all." BANG! The door was slammed shut on a source of applicants that could be a good one. What happened in the past that soured you on employment services? Whose fault was it that the applicants sent over for interview were far from acceptable? You probably did what most sales managers do when working with an employment service. You called a particular agency (or even more than one), you stated your need for a sales representative, offered a few details, such as salary, expenses, company car, and size of territory, and then sat back for this avalanche of highly qualified individuals. But the avalanche never came, did it? A few warm bodies were sent over to you for interview, and after you turned all of them down, they stopped coming.

There are any number of good salespeople who register with an employment service—some because they are still working and would rather have someone else do the searching for them and others because they know that more ground can be covered for them in less time. Don't accept the fallacious generality that the only people who go to an employment agency are those who are too lazy to look for a job for themselves. That's ridiculous. The truth is that the smarter individuals know that an agency has many job openings to choose from and that the details are there. It's much quicker than chasing down jobs one at a time. And really, isn't this the type of individual you want? One who places a heavy premium on time—selling time?

There is a way to get the most out of the services offered by an employment agency. Like so many other situations, your input will determine the quality of the output. Don't place a job order with an employment service on the telephone. Instead, call personally at the office and meet the employment counselor who will handle your job order. Bring with you a detailed position description, all the possible details of the job in writing, a brochure on your company benefits, a descriptive brochure on your company, and a sampling of your product literature. (Also, a few copies of your annual report, if yours is a public company.) Now look what's happened. The employment counselor knows you, knows what you are like and exactly what kind of individual is apt to please you. Furthermore, the counselor is now familiar with your company and has enough information and material to be able to *sell* your company to the applicant in short order. And if you have done a good job of impressing the counselor on exactly how much quality you expect in an applicant, you will have avoided the possibility of being sent individuals who are below the standards you have set forth.

The world's largest employment service, Snelling and Snelling, which has some six-hundred offices throughout the United States and in South America, places salesmen in companies of all sizes on a daily basis. Every office has a sales desk operated by a professional employment counselor who knows what makes salespeople tick. They are trained constantly to provide the best possible service to employers. But the sales managers who get the most out of these counselors are those who fortify them with the details, the literature, and the information that helps sell the job to the applicant. And if those of us in selling agree that there's nothing like personal contact when conveying information about a product, why do we, in the process of recruiting, attempt to work with an employment service counselor strictly by telephone and expect results of high quality? There's nothing like personal contact. We must never forget that. I happen to know that the Snelling and Snelling system, for one, never allows an applicant to go on an interview without first being given a *personal* interview by a counselor to determine if the individual is the type who can qualify for the job.

Are College Placement Bureaus a Failure?

You or your company may be regularly sending letters to college placement bureaus in those parts of the country where territories are hard to fill. Or you may be sending them to all major colleges in the hope that good applicants will be willing to relocate. In either case, you wonder what happens to all this literature. Does it end up in the right hands, in the right place? How come we don't get more applications through this avenue? Why, when we arrive to conduct interviews on campus, do so few applicants report? Sometimes none at all. Is it because no one wants a sales position? Do they *all* consider selling debasing? Is it an exercise in futility?

It doesn't have to be. In fact, it can be productive. It just doesn't work too well by mail—or by phone, for that matter. There are two problems to be bucked. First of all, it is true that most college students who are about to graduate and face the world want no part of a selling job.

The reasons are many. The major one, of course, is that our higher institutions of learning instill in those taking up business courses that they will be marketers or even sales managers upon graduation. Selling, according to academia, is still something that just about anyone can do. Wrong as that attitude definitely is, it's there. It's something to be reckoned with. The other problem is equally frustrating. Placement directors at our colleges are generalists in the true sense of the word. They know a little about every industry and every position in it and a lot about no specific industry or its jobs. They are much like the personnel managers found in industry who recruit everything from a janitor to a comptroller, yet their greatest fund of knowledge lies in policies, benefits, labor relations, etc. Under these conditions, therefore, how can we expect to send a nice letter with attractive literature to an individual whose desk is loaded with similar incoming mail and hope that this feeble exercise will produce top-quality individuals who are raring to go within the sales force for which we are recruiting? No way. It just doesn't happen.

If you want some good, positive results from college placement directors, *call on them.* As a field sales manager, you do a lot of traveling, you're almost everywhere. From time to time you're in the back yards of colleges that will graduate many young people who could be sold the idea of joining your company. Take a little time and stop in. Shake the hands of placement directors, get to know them, sell your company to them, impress upon them how great an opportunity you have in store for graduates who qualify; leave literature, job description, details, the works. Then, back at the home office, write them a letter. Thank them for their time and send them more company and product literature. One set is never enough at a school. Some students will borrow it and never return it. Tell them you will send them more when needed. Then stay in touch with them. Phone them periodically and ask when interviews will be lined up. Make sure that your interviews are scheduled for the morning of the first day they start interviewing if possible. If not, in the morning of subsequent days. But always in the morning. People are brighter then and more impressionable. You will be one of the very few sales managers that placement directors know. All the others are names on correspondence or voices over the telephone. You, however, are a person. Someone they have met or even had lunch with. They will know more about your company than any other company, including the huge corporations—only because they know you.

Any college or university that has a school of business or school of management where marketing is taught can be an excellent source of applicants for you. Keep in mind that the state university at Memphis, Tennessee, and Lansing Community College in Lansing, Michigan, are the only schools in the nation with majors in salesmanship.

Were All Bases Touched?

There is always a territory that seems to remain empty more often than not. It may be in a general area where applicants are very scarce. And it may be hard to transfer people into it because it's not the most desirable place in which to live. You probably have such a territory. Even if it is presently filled, you worry about the tenure of the person covering it. But the word *worry* is the one to focus on. When we worry, we do so mentally, never verbally. We think about our worries and rarely talk about them.

In recruiting, in addition to doing the normal things that bring in applicants, the oldest device of them all—word of mouth—is often forgotten. It's a base that sales managers forget to touch. You need a sales representative. You need this person now, for a difficult-to-fill territory. Why not make a list of the many people you could tell and keep it on your desk as a reminder? Whom to include? Tell your friends, customers, neighbors, suppliers, office staff, sales staff, the house organ editor, the public relations department, and as many passing strangers as you can. In other words, don't just keep your search a secret; tell everyone. You never know who knows someone who could fit the bill and do it well.

I once found a great salesman for a hard-to-fill territory simply because I stopped and chatted with our telephone operators at the home office and planted the seed. Within a week I received a phone call from an experienced salesman who was the second cousin of a friend of a neighbor of one of our telephone operators. Isn't it amazing how the message had been transmitted through so many people? On another occasion I obtained a lead through a taxi driver on an individual who was looking for sales work. At the end of a conversation that was restricted to the upcoming presidential election I simply threw in, "Do you happen to know anyone who is looking for a sales job?" He did.

Results through the word-of-mouth technique should not surprise you. Think of what happens whenever a rumor is started. How long does it really take before dozens of people know about it and are repeating it to dozens of others? I'm not suggesting that there is as much intrigue in word-of-mouth recruiting as there is in the spreading of rumors, but it certainly has its place in the recruiting process.

Are Interviews Tedious?

Ho-hum. How tedious this job of interviewing is. How many times have you said this, or at least thought it? Have you noticed how differently each interview goes? How sometimes you can get to the point very quickly and with others it takes forever? Remember John Smith, the fellow you interviewed a few weeks ago? You didn't like him from the moment he stepped into your office, and yet you reluctantly spent forty-five minutes with him. Is this why you have been postponing the conducting of interviews for applicants, because you know it's going to take so much of your time? Have you been looking for an interviewing checklist to be followed throughout the process? Have you discovered yet that a good one really doesn't exist? Did you notice how your own personnel manager, an expert in the field, himself admits that interviews vary all over the lot? Maybe this conversation rings a bell!

"I see that you went to New York University and majored in marketing."

"That's right."

"My neighbor, Jim Bosworth, is an NYU grad, too. Do you happen to know him?"

"Gee, no, I don't."

"Oh, well, it's a big place, and anyway he's older than you are. I see that you're married and have two children."

"That's right, sir."

"And you spent two years in the army."

"Yes, sir."

On and on it goes. What a complete waste of time for both you and the applicant. Do you realize what's really happening here? You are virtually reading back to the applicant what the applicant wrote for your benefit—and asking if it's correct. Why would it be incorrect? What a silly exercise. It all happens because you were too busy and too rushed to have given some serious thought to the techniques of interviewing, which can be handled skillfully. Actually, the interview represents a golden opportunity to find out what makes a person tick. It is a test that an applicant must pass in order to receive any further consideration. It is a *selling* situation wherein you, the buyer, are observing and evaluating the product, the applicant.

Far too many sales executives are still observing the rules of decades ago! Be kind to the nervous applicant. Place all applicants at ease. Start off with some small talk. Be considerate, etc. Come on—let's face it. If applicants are nervous and so introverted that they do a poor job of selling themselves at an interview, how well are they going to sell your products?

Let's understand one thing! To find good salespeople, you sometimes literally have to wade through a regiment of mediocrity. Time should be more valuable to you than ever before, and the rules have certainly changed substantially.

Observations pertaining to the individual's poise, personality, and habits should begin immediately upon the applicant's entrance into your office. Handling people in a certain way will bring out the traits that you want to observe. For instance, don't offer to take a person's hat and coat or even suggest what should be done with them.

If the person is sharp, the matter will be handled smoothly and without comment. If the applicant is extra sharp, such garments will have been left outside your office. Then don't make an effort to shake hands. See if the applicant takes the initiative. A good salesperson is aware of the warmth and value of a handshake and knows exactly how to execute it in a smooth fashion. Note if he or she sits down before being asked to do so. Observe the manner in which the applicant sits in the chair. If you are interviewing someone with much selling sense, you will note that this person will sit up alertly and project a businesslike attitude. When applicants light up a cigarette on their own or ask permission to smoke, ask them if they smoke while selling. (This is a very poor habit in the prospect's or customer's office, and certainly when selling oneself.)

When you interviewed John, did you know exactly what to ask before he entered your office? Or did you play it by ear? Playing it by ear is another way of saying, "I didn't bother to prepare." What to ask the applicant during an interview should not be a problem. Not if during the preliminary evaluation you made marginal notes on the resume in an attempt to read between the lines. How and when you ask these questions, however, is something else. Naturally, you could easily work them in at the appropriate time during the course of the interview. But this attitude is in consonance with the theory that you must spend at least a half hour with each applicant. Not so. Spending time with a person who doesn't impress you may promote goodwill for your company, but it does absolutely nothing for your territorial needs. Your job is to find good sales representatives as quickly as possible.

Leave most of the "good-willing" to your public relations department at the home office.

Your questions, therefore, should come at the very beginning of the interview. The important factor is that you take *full charge*, with rapid-fire questioning, placing the applicant immediately on the defensive. The rationale? To see how long it takes individuals to lift themselves out of such a hole and diplomatically take control of the interview by asking *you* some questions. When, during the sales call, the prospect or customer begins with a barrage of how much better the competition is, does the sales representative wait until the hole is too deep to come out of, or is some action taken early in the game to regain control of the selling situation? Isn't it the same here? Wouldn't you expect that to be a trait easily observed rather than lacking?

You say that many times resumes are quite complete. So much so that it's hard to read between the lines, and it's quite difficult to come up with questions such as we're suggesting here. Well, try some of these:

- How many sales calls are you accustomed to making in one day?
- What do you feel your real potential is?
- Why do you want to work for us?
- What do you know about us?
- What makes you think that you would be successful with this company?
- What book or article have you read on salesmanship lately?
- How would you define salesmanship?
- What selling technique seems to work best for you?

If the applicant is able to survive your barrage, you have a promising individual with whom more time will be well spent.

Then, are you sure you're closing the interview properly? Are you the kind, gentle soul who takes the last five minutes or more to explain what's going to happen next, what the company policy is in the selection of applicants, how long it will take to come up with some decisions, etc., etc? Well, the closing of an interview can be extremely significant when it is used to test the applicant's own closing techniques. And you save a lot of time in the process. Never offer an explanation of what the next step will be. Simply stand up, hold out your hand and thank the individual for coming in for an interview. If the applicant shakes hands and leaves without asking what you think, chances are that that person wouldn't ask for the order when selling your product. A startling revelation, isn't it?

You say, "This is terrible, I might lose a good sales representative by this treatment, this type of closing." Well, what happened to your control? In the event that you are very impressed with an applicant who does fail to ask when your decision will be made—and you want to pardon this only flaw—ask the applicant to phone you in a few days or whenever you think you'll be in a position to give even a preliminary answer. By so doing, you place the burden on the applicant. No call back, no further consideration. Too tough? Not at all. The applicant who fails to call you either doesn't want the job or is not good at following through. In either case you haven't lost a thing. You don't want to have to *sell* the job to an applicant *after* an interview, and the one who is poor at following through is the same individual who fails to get back to the prospect or customer with a quotation, a quantity price, a question on a product, etc.

I hasten to point out that these interviewing techniques are not theoretical. Far from it. For the first twelve years of the quarter century I've spent in sales management I was a sales manager in the pharmaceutical industry. It was hard to find good applicants, even harder to find people who even qualified (they had to be pharmacists or hold degrees in chemistry, physiology, premed, etc.). We had a sales force of over five-hundred. In that period I must have interviewed several thousand applicants, always using these techniques. And they worked. They saved me loads of time. There were instances when I'd interview as many as fifteen people in one day. Those who couldn't stand my aggressive questioning or didn't jump in and question me didn't last. Within ten minutes I'd be standing up, shaking their hands, and politely dismissing them. But those who showed poise and aggressiveness of their own got a thorough interview, sometimes as long as forty-five minutes. Rest assured that those who survived and were hired were capable enough to cope with the druggists and physicians we called on. None of this looking up to them and always keeping them on a pedestal. We had excellent products. The benefits derived from them were fantastic. What was there to be timid about?

Yes, these interviewing techniques may sound unusually tough, but when handled properly they help you weed out the real sales-minded people from those who *think* that they belong in sales work. And isn't that what it's all about? How well I recall my succeeding years in the Lacy Institute when I'd be interviewing applicants for client companies, many of them for jobs in sales management. It was a recruiting and screening process. The top three would be recommended to the client for final consideration and selection. And I never ceased to be amazed at how many of these applicants would answer all the questions posed—and never ask any of their own. Not even the name of the company for which they were being interviewed. If they didn't ask, I simply wouldn't tell them, and they would leave as happy as clams. And I often wondered how their conversations would go that evening at the dinner table:

> *Wife:* Were you on time for your interview today dear?
> *Applicant:* Oh, yes. In fact I was five minutes early.
> *Wife:* Good. How did it go?
> *Applicant:* Very well, dear.
> *Wife:* What company was it for?
> *Applicant:* Well, er, I really don't know.
> *Wife:* You don't know???

How could you blame her if, at that point, she tipped the table over on him.

It's sad, I will admit, but that's the way it is. As a sales manager, your job is not to massage the ego of applicants who just don't make it, but rather to weed out those who qualify—and in the least possible time. Interviewing is too important a function to approach it lightly. Look at it this way: You regularly spend 5 to 10 percent of your time interviewing. (If you don't, you should. Even when all of the territories are filled, you should be interviewing people who are looking for a change and thereby developing a bullpen. You never know when your next opening will occur. It could be while you're reading this.) If your interviewing techniques are disorganized and very time-consuming, you will find yourself spending as much as 50 to 75 percent of your time on such activities every time you have an opening. As a result, at years end your sales figures will have suffered because you didn't have the time to supervise properly, train, and motivate the best of your sales staff.

Does Grading Applicants Become Confusing?

You recently interviewed Mary Smith. You decided that she's a good applicant. What's a good applicant? What does that statement really mean? Let's take it one step further. How does one determine the difference between a good applicant and an excellent applicant? Is there a tally sheet? Is there a grading system? There has to be. And it need not be complicated, ultrasophisticated, computerized, or psychologically oriented.

When it's all said and done, the telltale signs of a good applicant can be narrowed down to seven. They are personality, poise, speaking voice, appearance, attitude, interest in the position, and the speed with which the applicant thinks. Imagine how easy the so-called grading can become if, immediately after interviewing an individual you were to take a grading sheet (see below) and, while the person is still very fresh in your mind, you quickly circle the appropriate grades. Then, after inserting any specific comments, you would circle *Very desirable, Desirable,* or *Not desirable* in accordance with the column containing the most circles. Oversimplified? Perhaps. But think of the value of this time-saving grading sheet, which gets stapled on top of each resume. When you begin to narrow down the applicants you have interviewed in an attempt to arrive at the best three, or the best two, or the individual who is going to get the nod, the grading sheet greatly helps to evaluate and categorize individuals without having to dip back into your own powers of retention in an attempt to remember each applicant and what impressed you most.

GRADING SHEET

Applicant _____

(Circle one)

Qualifications:	Excellent	Good	Fair
Personality	E	G	F
Poise	E	G	F
Speaking voice	E	G	F
Appearance	E	G	F
Attitude	E	G	F
Interest	E	G	F
Thinks	Fast	Av.	Slow

Comments:

Grade:	Very desirable	Desirable	Not desirable

If the policy in your company is to have the desirable applicants also interviewed by another member of the sales management staff (sometimes several members), don't attach your grading sheet. Instead, give each interviewer a blank sheet for the purpose of grading the applicant without knowledge of what appears on your own sheet. You can rest assured that a comparison of the grading sheets will be most helpful in making the final selection.

Did You Lose the Best Applicant?

Do you recall Bill Phantom? Every field sales manager encounters a Bill Phantom here and there. This is a guy who reports for an interview, impresses the sales manager in every conceivable way, asks for the job, grills the sales manager as to when the decision will be made, and then leaves. Never to be heard from again. What's even worse, when you finally decide that he is really the best person you interviewed and you try to contact him, he's nowhere to be found. No answer at home, morning, noon, or night. No longer employed. You almost begin to panic. Here is the best one of the lot, and he can't be reached. He's lost, and you can't wait forever. Reluctantly you say, "I'll have to settle for second best."

The phantom need not be a phantom at all. After a round of interviewing applicants, there should be what is known as the aftermath. By this we mean that period of time (one week to ten days) when we sit back and wait for the ones who have been graded as very desirable to take the next step. As a matter of fact, you should take a sheet of paper, call it the Aftermath Sheet, and record on it which applicants phoned you, when, did they ask for the job again, and how you left it. Why should you be the aggressor who chases down the applicant? If the person seeking a job with your organization is aggressive enough to stay on top of you for an answer, then here again you have someone who will be aggressive in selling the product or service that you market. It is not at all unusual for someone who has been graded as very desirable to be completely taken out of the running because one week to ten days have gone by and not one word has been heard from that individual. You see, in the aftermath you discovered that Bill Phantom was not that aggressive after all.

Recruiting can be more fun than it really is, and more productive in the process. It is all a case of strategy, common sense, and a thorough understanding of the various aspects connected with interviewing and the many avenues through which applicants can be found.

8
The Selection Process

How confused you became when you looked over the results of both the psychological and the aptitude tests given to the best three applicants from the group you interviewed. One applicant came out smelling like a rose from an aptitude standpoint, but psychologically he was termed "unstable." Another seemed to do well in both areas but was still termed a *fair risk*. The third was a complete disappointment from a testing standpoint. And yet, as far as you were concerned, that was the best applicant of the three. You pondered over what to do. You discussed the results of the tests with your superiors. They had trouble getting back to you with their opinions because of their heavy travel schedules. In the meantime, all three found other jobs, and you were left with no one. Now you had to start looking all over again.

Are Test Results Useful?

This problem of testing is a big one. So much has been written on the subject, both pro and con, that one wonders exactly which way to turn. There is no question that the statement "Testing is nothing more than a management tool" is a valuable one. Tests are tools that can guide you into making a decision. But they can also prove frustrating. Especially when the results so greatly contradict your own conclusions about an applicant.

After researching this subject for years—and I can assure you that every possibility was taken into consideration—I have come to the conclusion that in sales work, testing is not as valuable as in other areas. What do you measure in salespeople when you test them? When people take exams for certification or for positions with companies in scientific and professional areas, the amount of knowledge and skill possessed can to a great degree be measured. But in sales work this is not the case. It has been argued by some competent authorities that psychological makeup is an important aspect of selling. That's why psychological tests have been touted for years. Yet, there are examples upon examples whereby an individual who has been very successful in sales work has tested as unstable from a psychological standpoint. There are those who claim that it takes a special breed of cat to succeed in selling. That special breed, they say, is someone who is able to live more with fantasy than with reality. It appears that the confirmed optimist does better in selling than the realistic pessimist. So where do you go from there?

Then there are tests that, through mechanical, mathematical, and logistical problems, claim to test an individual's sense of good reasoning. But good reasoning is not always an important factor in sales success. Tell a sales representative that a particular product cannot be sold in a certain territory and see what happens. He'll go out and prove you wrong. He'll make sales that you never thought possible.

Any astute student of salesmanship would tell you that the basic fundamental ingredient considered most important in a sales applicant is personality. If a person has a sales-oriented personality as a foundation upon which to build good selling techniques, almost everything else becomes secondary. It is a known fact that people sell through their personalities. It is also a known fact that if the personality of the salesperson is right, prospects and customers will listen. But if the personality is in any way abrasive, the chances of making a sale are reduced most substantially. Under these circumstances, what good are sophisticated tests that are far afield from this vital area?

Some fifteen years ago we developed, at the Lacy Institute, a simple test to do one thing, and one thing alone. It was designed to measure how an applicant thinks as a salesperson. Indirectly, of course, it revealed the individual's personality. To this day, after having been used over twenty thousand times, it still seems to do the job as thoroughly as anything else. I don't know of any other similar test in existence, but certainly that does not mean that they are not available. The only point that I am making is that save for this type of test, little else remains that can be considered of specific value from a testing standpoint.

I shall never forget a survey we conducted after this test

had been administered over ten thousand times. It disclosed many unusual findings, but one was a shocker— at least to me it was. The results showed that 67 percent of people connected with selling are introverts. At that time I found this very hard to believe. But since that day I have found that this percentage can be considered a very valuable statistic. In case you disagree, just make a little survey of your own. In so doing, you will find that two out of three salespeople will:

- Never sit in the front row at a function, meeting, gathering, or whatever.
- Never float around at a cocktail party to make new friends. They are satisfied to stay with people they know, in a corner, for the duration of the party.
- Rarely walk up to a stranger and introduce themselves. They usually let it happen after a certain amount of conversation for the necessary warm-up.
- Rarely run for the presidency of an organization. They claim they don't want the extra work, but really they don't want to step up to the podium and run the meeting.
- Rarely return an item that was sold to them on a final-sale basis. They rationalize that they knew it was a final sale when they purchased the item. The real reason is that they are not extroverted enough to make the attempt to get their money back.

I once asked a very successful sales manager, Ben Nechis of Endo Laboratories, if he tested applicants before hiring them for sales positions. His answer was simple. He said, "I don't test them, I smell them." I expressed surprise and wonderment. He explained. He said, "To me, testing is most confusing. I discovered long ago that, through experience, I developed a nose for individuals who have the right type of personality for sales work. That's why I claim that I smell them. Give me five minutes with an applicant and I'll be able to make a judgment. I'm not always right, but then, who is? More often than not, however, my nose does not fail me. If in five minutes of conversation I find the person's personality stimulating to me, I assume that it will be equally stimulating to the prospects and customers. If the opposite is the case, I go on the the next applicant."

His words were far from scientifically oriented. But the success of his company is public record.

Does Reference Checking Seem Fruitless?

You feel completely fed up with the process of checking references. You know that you have to, because it's company policy. You also know that you should. After all, an applicant doesn't always tell you the *real* truth. There are many times when important facts are hidden. Of course, you always hope that you can uncover such facts through reference checking. And you set out to do just that.

But why is it that you never learn anything that you didn't already know about an applicant? How come people talk in generalities when they discuss a previous employee? "It's a waste of time," you say, "and I'm tempted to give up the whole idea."

Your feelings are very common among sales managers. So much so that some sales managers will entrust this task to a secretary. And that's always disastrous. The moment the secretary admits that she's checking references for her boss, the party's over. Nothing of value is ever learned. Let's tackle this problem head on. More often than not the reason you hate to get involved in checking references is because you consider it a tedious, unexciting task that is usually fruitless. The problem could very well be attitudinal with you. Perhaps if you became more skillful at reference checking and you uncovered many more situations to broaden your knowledge about an applicant, the task would not seem so tedious. It could even become exciting for you. Especially when you become so skillful that you are able to get people to really open up and tell you what ordinarily might have never been disclosed.

First of all, as you can already assume, the best way to check references is by telephone. For obvious reasons. People always refrain from placing anything in writing that would be damaging to an individual's reputation or chances for future employment. They simply don't want to get involved to that degree, particularly since they are well aware that it could lead to a lawsuit. And you can understand that, I'm sure.

On the other hand, a significant verbal statement made during a friendly conversation will many times slip out, damaging or not, even though the original intention may have been to say nothing. It takes skill to draw people out. You have that skill, since you regularly are able to draw applicants out when interviewing them. You just never considered the possibility of applying that very same skill in the process of reference checking.

Let's take it step by step. There are specific rules to be followed when you become engaged in reference checking and want to do it creatively.

- Never check a reference by contacting the personnel department of a company. The person who responds is only in a position to verify dates of employment, positions held, etc. The candidate's proficiency or ability to get along with others is rarely known about in the personnel office of a good-sized company.
- Always concentrate your efforts in reaching the immediate supervisor of the candidate. That person, if approached properly, will be happy to chat about the former employee and give you information over and above work performance, such as dependability, degree of cooperativeness, team spirit, etc. Why will this information be given to you happily? Simply because you are talking to someone in the same ball park that you are in—sales management. That supervisor knows exactly what you're going through. Has been in your shoes many times. Doesn't want you to get stuck with someone who'll make your life miserable. The same cooperation would be expected of you if the situation were reversed.
- Make sure that you ask about strengths and weaknesses. These are almost never revealed in a resume, and even if they have been discussed during your interview with the applicant, the real truth is sometimes very hard to nail down. You see what you're doing? You are leading the conversation. You are asking specific questions, not simply saying, "What can you tell me about this person?"

- React enthusiastically to the answers given you by your counterpart. You are asking for opinions. Human nature is such that people always feel important when asked for their opinions. However, upon hearing these opinions, be sure you express surprise, concern, or whatever the case may be, but with an enthusiastic voice. This always encourages people to go into even greater detail.
- Always have a telephone reference checklist before you when phoning for references. (A sample copy is found at the end of this section.) The sequence of the questions asked is important, as is the completeness of the reference checking.

You may be wondering what happens when an applicant has been fired or has left the company under adverse conditions. Is it not best just to forget reference checking altogether? Not so. It is a known fact that a good applicant may have been fired by one company and yet have all of the qualities that will help bring about success in another. Certainly it is a problem, without question. But not an insurmountable one. Just make sure you don't give up too easily and do no checking in situations of this nature.

Occasionally you'll come across an individual who's totally unwilling to give you any information on a former employee. It may be a means of taking the "easy way out," or it may be company policy not to divulge such information. A good technique, when this occurs, is to accept the reason given but to ask to speak to that person's superior. If that fails, go to the next step, assuming that it's possible. Experience has regularly shown that the higher an individual is on the organizational chart, the more cooperative the reaction to reference checking.

Because of the Federal Privacy Act, it is a must that you have every applicant sign a disclosure statement before anything is done regarding reference checking. This statement should be routinely signed at the beginning of the first interview or when the applicant is completing your application form. In addition to complying with federal law, the signing of this statement has an additional benefit. It will make an applicant realize that references *will* be checked, thus promoting more truthfulness throughout the interview. If an applicant outrightly refuses to sign a disclosure statement, still another purpose has been served. There may well be severe problems in the applicant's background, and a great deal of your time has been saved.

Obviously, if the reason for not signing is because the applicant is presently working and doesn't want his employer to know that he is looking for a better position, there is room for discussion. In such cases, you simply explain that you will definitely not contact the present employer but that you still need the authority, in writing, to contact other previous employers or certain individuals known to the applicant.

Once you get a good handle on what might be termed *creative* reference checking, this part of your job will not prove to be as boring as it has been in the past. In fact, you'll be amazed at the many interesting conversations you will become involved in with other sales managers in other companies and in other industries. You will end up comparing notes on a myriad of things, and there is certainly nothing wrong with that. We all know that we learn something from everyone with whom we come in contact.

TELEPHONE REFERENCE CHECKLIST

Applicant _____

Company . . . .
Company Repre. Name . . . . Title . . . .
Was in your employ from . . . . to . . . .
Why did he/she leave? . . . .
. . . .
How would you rate this person's sales ability? . . . .
. . . .
. . . .
Why do you say that? . . . .
. . . .
What would you say his/her strong points are? . . . .
. . . .
In what areas would you say he/she needed improvement? . . . .
. . . .
How about getting along with others? . . . .
. . . .
Any special problem or other information you can give
me that would be helpful? . . . .
. . . .
. . . .

DISCLOSURE STATEMENT

I understand that an investigative report may be obtained by you in order to enable you to evaluate me as a prospective employee. This investigative report may include information concerning my character, general reputation, personal characteristics, mode of living, and financial responsibility.

I further understand that I have the right to make a request to you to learn the complete nature and scope of this investigative report.

I hereby acknowledge that I have read and received a copy of this statement and hereby authorize you to obtain an investigative report as described above.

Date.............. Signature..............

Did Your First Choice Accept Another Job?

What disappointment you experienced when, after going through eighteen applicants, selecting the top three, and offering the position to the best of the three, you lost her. You had gone through all of the necessary paperwork, all of the necessary approvals, all of the forms had been filled out, and you made the offer. What happened? She politely informed you that she had accepted another job. You then had to scurry to get to your second choice.

You probably rationalized your predicament by saying, "Well, it was probably fate. Maybe she wasn't as good as I thought she was. It was not in the cards." The truth of the matter is that this happens over and over again to many, many sales managers. And it happens because of one specific aspect of the selection process. Timing.

First of all, if you keep timing in mind, much can be done to avoid this pitfall at the end of the selection process. It revolves around the order in which the eighteen candidates were interviewed. Whether we like to face it or not, when interviewing applicants, we are always comparing one with another. Since this is a known fact, it makes much sense to interview applicants according to how they "stack up" on paper. It is quite possible, you will agree, to arrive at some degree of interest in an individual by what has been written in his or her application or resume, or both. From this degree of interest you should arrive at a sequence for interviewing. In other words, interview the person who is least interesting first and leave the most promising applicant for last. In doing so, not only do you get sharper at interviewing as you go along in the process, but you will be able to make a much more significant comparison of the more promising people with those already interviewed and who are not quite as promising.

The advantage of this procedure is that as soon as you are through with your last interview, you can begin to take *swift* action regarding a decision as to the person who will be your first choice for a job offer. Timing is now on your side, provided of course that you never forget the importance of moving rapidly toward making the job offer and getting a commitment. Rapidly—because good applicants never last. A person who has applied to you for a sales job, if totally sales minded, will also have applied to several other companies at the same time. As we all know, a good sales representative never stops after having made x number of calls in any one day. The more calls, the more possibilities of making sales. The same is true when this type of individual is looking for a sales job. Not to accept this means not to recognize the better choices among the candidates who applied.

Now, having arrived at your first choice, waste no time. If you don't have to go through calisthenics with the home office to gain approval or counter-approval by one or more individuals, take the necessary action at once and inform the individual of your job offer. If there are other people involved in making a decision, press for it. Reach the individuals by phone. Explain how excited you are about this particular applicant. Explain particularly how this applicant compared so favorably over all the others that you interviewed. Finally, bring out the urgency by reminding the individuals concerned that a high-caliber applicant of this type just doesn't last, and you don't want to lose the opportunity of hiring this person. When this last type of statement is made in a very positive and strong fashion to your associates or superiors, they are able to realize that they may be causing you to lose the applicant if they waste time in giving you their stamp of approval. In any event, do whatever you can. You must constantly bear in mind that losing good applicants is usually attributable to their having found another situation and accepted it because you didn't move as quickly as the other company did. And you can understand why an applicant would abandon you for the company that moves more quickly. In the applicant's mind, the fast-moving company is more dynamic, and growth will come much more swiftly. Your company, in the mind of the applicant, moves too slowly—so why wait for a job offer, which may not even come, and lose other, more exciting opportunities in the meantime?

Did Your Job Offer Excite the Applicant?

After weighing all of the variables, you arrived at your first choice and you decided to make the job offer. You phoned the individual, made the job offer, expected a yes with excitement—but you didn't get it. Instead, the applicant said, "Sounds good, but I'll have to think about it and get back to you." The best you could do, under those circumstances, was to pin the person down as to when you would hear. Better still, you stated emphatically that you needed to know in the next three days.

Why does this happen? you ask yourself, as you hang up. After all, the applicant had been asked whether, if the job offer was made, an acceptance would come about. The answer to that one was a definite yes. So, why at this juncture, is there much to be thought about? Why wasn't the applicant more excited upon hearing of the job offer?

Well, like many other things in life, when a job offer finally comes, you wonder if it's the job for you. This is a human reaction. Can you change this reaction in any way? You certainly can. You do so by the way in which you present the job offer. I learned a long time ago why applicants didn't react with much excitement when I phoned them with a job offer. After thinking about it, I realized how obvious the answer was. The applicant, upon hearing your voice on the telephone, knows immediately that a job offer is about to be made. Why not? If you were turning down the applicant, you would do so by letter. The usual "Dear John" letter. If you are phoning, it's because you are about to make a job offer. So, you couch it in the best terms that you know how, and by the time you've actually come out with the words that constitute the job offer, the excitement is no longer there. It is received almost in a matter-of-fact fashion, and this leaves you so bewildered that you wonder if perhaps you have made the job offer to the wrong individual.

Here is a solution to this problem. And it works. Never phone an applicant to make a job offer. Instead, send a telegram. That's much more impressive. Besides, the image of a telegram is world renowned. It is important and it always brings about a sense of urgency. I have found the best wording to be as follows:

Congratulations. You have been selected, as our first choice, for the New England sales position. Please confirm your acceptance in writing immediately. Best wishes for growth and success in our organization.

Not only does the applicant get excited by having received a job offer via telegram, but the "immediate written acceptance" request almost suggests that there is a second choice waiting in the wings and that there is no time to lose. All I can tell you is that it works. In fact, many salespeople told me after joining the organization that the telegram gave them the feeling that they were joining a "gung-ho" outfit. In several instances, applicants who had received job offers by letter from one or two other companies were completely swayed when the telegram arrived.

It may sound like a very small thing, but it isn't. A job offer is important to the person receiving it. Why not have it arrive in a dramatic fashion—by telegram? It's not that expensive, and it makes a lot of sense.

Did the Person You Hired Have a Change of Mind?

At last you breathe a sigh of relief. You will not have to recruit for a while, you happily remind yourself. You have just hired the individual who will fill your last open territory. You now have a full complement of salespeople in your district. But the phone rings, and the last person you hired is on the other end of the line. You are apologetically told that the successful applicant has had a change of mind. All plans are off.

What can you do to change the picture around? How can you convince this person that the first decision, the one that would bring completeness to your district, was the better one and that it should be stuck to—at all costs? The answer is, you don't. That would be the wrong solution to the problem if, in fact, it's a solution at all.

Experience has shown over and over again that to sell a job to an applicant the second time around, is a mistake. The enthusiasm displayed by the applicant during the first interview, continued throughout the second interview and further displayed when acceptance of the job offer came about, must be genuine. If it is, the change of mind rarely comes about. On the other hand, if the enthusiasm is manufactured, a change of heart is not too hard to come by. In any event, to resell a position is a dangerous undertaking. It's almost like encouraging turnover. The individual reaccepts the job offer with the attitude "It better be as good a deal as I have been told." This is tantamount to a very negative attitude. And it carries over into all facets of the selling process by the individual. Big sales are expected to happen rather than be brought about creatively. Each time they don't happen, a specific thought crosses the mind of that individual. The inner voice says, "I knew I shouldn't have allowed myself to be talked into this situation." The result is that more often than not the association turns out to be short-lived.

Generally speaking, when the person you have hired has a change of mind, it is best to offer congratulations on whatever other endeavor has won out and go on to your second choice of the placement process—if that person is still available. This may sound, to some degree, like a defeatist attitude. You may feel that as long as the individual is salvageable, the challenge should be met and that you should put your best salesmanship to work. Although such a reaction is understandable, and even commendable, it is too dangerous. The odds are against you. You may as well know it and avoid bitter disappointment of larger proportions later on.

There is something you can do to avoid this unfortunate happening. It does not always work, but it is certainly worth trying for the number of times that it does come to your rescue. Get a commitment from an individual as quickly as possible after the job offer. Your company may not use employment contracts for salespeople. This is understandable. Most of them don't work out. Yet, in the absence of a contract, there is such a thing as an employment letter. It is far from being as legally binding as a contract, if binding at all. But it does place the individual in a position of having to sign something, which constitutes a commitment of sorts. It is amazing how many individuals, once they have affixed their signature to something, will automatically refuse to consider a complete change of mind.

The contents of such an employment letter should be kept short and in simple language. After all, you don't want to make it look like a legal document. The letter will simply say that it is confirming the terms of the individual's employment and then goes on to reiterate the territory to be covered, the remuneration (broken down into its proper components such as salary, expenses, car allowance, etc.), the date that employment will commence, and any conditions of employment, such as completion of character references, credit checks, etc. Send the applicant an original with one copy, both of which have been signed by you, and request that the original be countersigned and returned to you. Now you have a commitment with a starting date in writing. I repeat, it doesn't mean all that much. Because of it you could never force anyone to report to work. Nor would you ever want to have a salesperson come to work under such circumstances. But at least you have done something psychological that most people hold dear. A promise has been made in writing, and it has been signed.

9

The Field Sales Manager's Personal Worries

Not too long ago you asked yourself some questions. You asked yourself if you were enjoying your job now as much as you did when you first became a field sales manager. You also asked yourself if the job hadn't become boring. After all, you mused, I'm doing the same things over and over again. I'm hiring, I'm replacing, I'm supervising, etc.

Is Your Job Rewarding?

This can be a problem with the field sales manager's job, but then again, it can be a problem with any job. There is always the possibility of being able to say, "I'm doing the same things over and over again."

But in sales management that is not really a true statement. In an assembly line, where an individual continually takes part A and connects it to part B and passes it along to the next person on the line, boredom is understandable. But in sales management it is not understandable. Here we are dealing with people. People are very different from each other. No two salespeople will react the same in any given situation. No two salespeople react the same to supervision. No two salespeople will sell the identical product in the same way. And these are the variables that make the job interesting. So, while it's true that the responsibilities of the job don't change and the duties of the job remain rather constant, the fact is that how these responsibilities and duties are discharged will usually take interesting avenues due to the people involved.

As an example, you will have to admit that no two interviewing sessions have ever been exactly alike. In my lifetime I have probably interviewed several thousand people for sales and sales management positions. It has never proved boring. I would never try to second-guess what an applicant will come up with. One never knows.

The same is true of field visits. After having made thousands of those, I am sure that no two of them were exactly alike. Really, when you think about it, sales management is perhaps the most exciting type of management in existence. You are not only dealing with salespeople, many of whom can be rather exciting, but you are also dealing with customers and with home office personnel and a host of other individuals with whom you will cross paths.

Perhaps the most common mistake made by a field sales manager is based on egotism. That's right. Your egotism many times will tell you that because you were promoted from a sales position to that of field sales manager, you are now in management. Well, that's true. However, you are far from top management, and while your position is usually referred to as middle management, let's be honest, it's not really in the middle but rather at the bottom of management. This is the first layer of management. This is the layer that is still carefully scrutinized by top management. Many a top management official looks at the field sales manager as an experiment. Particularly when the field sales manager was promoted from a selling job. We all know that a good salesperson does not always a good field sales manager make. So, at best, this is a trial period. A period in which everything you do is looked upon with much interest, not only because of what you did, but because of what it shows regarding your capabilities. It behooves you, therefore, not only to do as good a job as you are able but also to make as many contributions as you possibly can. You say, "How can I make contributions? The home office directs me to do this and to do that; it's all laid out on paper; the formulas are locked in. So, how can I contribute?" Well, it may seem as though everything is "locked in," but nothing ever is. There isn't a procedure, a rule, a policy, that can't be revised to make it better. The only problem is that few people work at it. Most people accept established procedures as law, abide by them, and don't think about how they could be changed for the better.

Here is a perfect example. When I was promoted to district sales manager in the pharmaceutical industry, it was with one of the larger companies. There is no question that the company was well organized. They had procedures for everything. They had an excellent training program at the home office. Perhaps the best in the industry. It lasted for six weeks. Imagine, for six weeks a salesperson was sent to New Jersey to learn about products, policies, salesmanship, and anything else that was considered critical. Now, six weeks is a long time, you will agree. Particularly since it meant attending class from nine to five, five days a week, with a few evening sessions thrown in. Since these classes were convened only about four times a year, if a field sales manager hired an individual between classes, it became a local responsibility to do some training before putting the individual out on territory. The home office had decided that this training would be conducted by the field sales manager in a hotel room in the town where the individual was hired and for one week's duration. The training was to consist of product knowledge. After all, how much could you do in one week? The products were many and varied, and quite technical in nature. Therefore, the entire week would have to be spent on product knowledge.

Now, this procedure had been going on for several years prior to my coming on the scene. I hired my first sales representative and then asked the home office to send me an agenda for the one-week's local training. To my surprise I was informed that there was no agenda. After all, I knew the products, I knew what had to be done, why was there need for an agenda?

I went ahead with the training job at hand, but I took many notes in the process. At the end of the week I reviewed in my mind what could have been done better, what products could have been given more time, etc., and then proceeded to develop an agenda for the next time. And I felt that it would be nice to send a copy to the home office. My boss sent me a glowing letter. He thought it was extremely creative and most innovative of me to have come up with an agenda. In fact, he thought it was so good that it was made a part of the field sales manager's manual so that all the other managers throughout the country would be following the same agenda.

The next individual I hired was trained according to my own agenda. By this time I had decided that it would be a good idea to administer a test at the end of the week just to see if the student had learned what the trainer had taught. I was pleased that my student obtained a grade ·of 92 percent. I thought it was important to send it to the home office for inclusion in the employee's personnel file. I also sent a copy to my boss. He flipped. He thought it was a *marvelous* idea to give people a test at the end of the one-week's field training period. And the same thing happened. It was made a part of the manual. Now everyone would use my test.

Now, there is nothing brilliant about me, nor was the company stupid. They were making a big profit. My only point in bringing this out is that we assume that there isn't much that can be done to improve upon the job at hand. Well, there is. It's simply a case of being aware of what is going on and being doubly aware of how the goings on could be made easier or better.

So, for these reasons I find it difficult to understand why some field sales managers will state, "The job is getting boring." Actually, it is so challenging a job that boredom is very, very rare. Whenever you are accomplishing a task through others, you become a psychologist by necessity, and this makes it all extremely interesting.

If, for some reason, you have thought or felt that your job is getting boring, there is a specific answer to this problem. You can easily straighten yourself out by realizing that your job is a fantastic training ground for top management. There is much consolation in the fact that most vice-presidents for sales and/or marketing have come up through the ranks. They started in sales, broke into management by becoming a field sales manager, and eventually landed a top management position in sales or marketing. When you think about it, there is no way that a vice-president for marketing could ever understand the problems of salespeople and field sales supervision without having been there. It's almost a necessity to come up through the ranks.

And if you want to stop being bored and are desirous of coming up through the ranks, then start today to be innovative. Look over everything your company is doing and consider how much you can improve upon it. In many instances you will work very hard and find no way that something can be improved upon. But as you proceed you *will* find a way to make a contribution. Maybe you can adjust something that is being done in the interviewing process. Maybe you can improve some of the forms. Maybe the field reporting forms don't contain all the information they could. Or perhaps they might contain information that's never used and could be easily discarded. Whatever the case, you *can* make a contribution.

No doubt, every so often after a long, hard day or after a long, grueling trip, you may have said to yourself, "I really question the rewards of this job." To think that way is a mistake. Your hours may be long and your job quite tedious, but the rewards are many. You may not see them on a daily basis, but they are there. Every time that you solve a problem, whether it be a sales problem or a personnel problem, you have broadened your scope and upgraded your capabilities. And as you climb the ladder of success, you may rest assured that you will fall upon your experiences of a field sales manager over and over again, each time realizing how much you did learn from all of them.

Is Your Future Insecure?

Particularly if you are a member of a large, national organization, you will probably every so often say to yourself, "My future is not clear." How do I know how long I will be a field sales manager? How do I know if and when I will be promoted? How do I know that anybody even knows exactly what I am accomplishing in the field?

These are all good questions and normal ones. But they are not terribly unusual. After all, whose future *is* clear? No one really knows what the future will hold. Most of us take the position that we should do the best job possible and the rest will take care of itself. In the main, that's very true. More often than not, the future pays off for people who paid in. So the better you perform in sales management, the more you are insuring your future. Is that all there is? you say. No, there's more.

Napoleon once said, "Circumstances? I make my own circumstances." Now that's a strong statement. Obviously, all of us cannot always make our own circumstances. Even Napoleon was not able to do so at all times. It's good that he had such a positive attitude, but strictly speaking, it was more of an attitude than a reality.

But let's talk about making our own circumstances. What can you do as a field sales manager to make sure that your future is better than the next field sales manager in the adjoining district? Well, the fact that you have read this book shows clearly that you're willing to invest in the future. You want to be better. You want to do your job as best as you possibly can. And if you study all of the problems and their solutions that have been thus far discussed you will have a substantial jump on your contemporaries by far. But there is one more aspect that I would like to bring to your attention. It's an aspect that helps you make your own circumstances. It is called *visibility*.

You see, there is no truer saying than "out of sight, out of mind." Positive proof of that is around us constantly. If you see someone on a daily basis, you never have any trouble remembering that person's name. But if you see someone once every three months, chances are that you will have a great deal of trouble remembering that person's name—if you are able to do so at all.

I'm sure you've noticed how a television star who appears on a regular show on a weekly basis develops a tremendous amount of fame. Such a star can hardly walk along the main street of any town without being accosted for autographs. Such a star is recognized instantly by just about everybody. Why? The visibility on national television has been extensive. But let that show be canceled and let that star be off the television screen for three, four, or five months, and see what happens. You'll probably say to a friend, "I haven't seen what's-his-name on television or doing anything else for a long time." Yes, "what's-his-name." You've already forgotten the name of the person you felt you knew so well. It doesn't take very long.

How does this apply to you? Look at it this way. You are management's representative out in the field. But you are not with management executives at the home office on a daily basis. In fact, think about how few times in the course of one year you are at the home office. If it's four, it's probably a lot. Think about something else that's even more frustrating. Many people at the home office will know you by name but isn't it amazing how, when you walk into the building, very few recognize you by sight? It's after you introduce yourself that they say, "Oh, yeah, Bill Jones from Chicago."

As you can see, in order to insure your future, you need more visibility than you ever realized. How do you get it? Well, you cannot be running to the home office at the drop of a hat. That could prove expensive and perhaps even annoying to your superiors. There should be a good reason for you to go to the home office. Otherwise, you belong in the field. But there is nothing in the book that says you cannot write, and write often. You can obtain a substantial amount of visibility through the memorandum route. Not only should you write a memorandum on every conceivable bit of communication that makes sense, but as you write such memos to your superiors, always send many copies. I don't mean indiscriminate copies, but copies to individuals that might have even a mild interest in the subject contained. For instance, if you're writing a memo about a quality control problem to your superior, even though you know it will be forwarded to the quality control department, send a copy to quality control, as well as market research, as well as product managers, and anyone else who might be interested in the particular problem involving a specific product.

And a good rule to follow, a basic one, is never to put more than one idea in a memorandum. This not only confuses the reader, but it also cuts down on your visibility. If you have three things to communicate about, write three different memos. And the opportunities are endless. Every time you make contact with one of your salespeople and you learn something that the home office might be interested in, write a memo. Every time you talk to a competitor or a customer or a prospect who tells you something that might be of interest to the home office, write a memo. Every time you see a competitive ad that you feel might not have been seen by people in the home office, write a memo. The opportunities are there. It's up to you to do something with them.

But might this not create the wrong impression? you ask. Might home office personnel decide that I do more writing of memos than managing of people? Could I be termed a nuisance? Not at all. I know where of I speak.

Back in 1951 I was hired by a large company. As a salesman, my opportunities of visiting the home office were extremely limited. Almost nonexistent. I was one of 325 sales representatives. I decided right then and there that I needed a great deal of visibility. I started writing memos. Fortunately, I could type. So, at least three times each week I would mail in a memorandum—with appropriate copies. Some weeks as many as five or six. Since the home office staff was very religious about answering correspondence, I would receive many answers from many people. Each time, however, it was quite significant to note the closing remarks. They would say something like, "Thank you for writing," "Thank you for communicating so well," "Thank you for keeping us so well informed." After four or five months the closing statements began to change somewhat. Instead of the usual thank you's, they would read as follows: "You certainly have your ear to the ground," "You are one of the very few who keeps the home office informed," "You are an astute individual who communicates well." You see what was happening? I was establishing a reputation. What's more, the statements were getting very flowery. People were becoming more and more impressed. They were even admitting that very few write in as often as I do.

Well, I did this for one solid year. And during that time I made sure that there was a constant rise in my sales curve. Then, unfortunately, I was recalled for the Korean conflict. But I decided then and there that this should not end my visibility. I knew my tour of duty would be for two years. I asked the home office to keep me on the mailing list for sales bulletins and new product information, including samples. They agreed. Each time I received a communication, I would write back with comments. Each month I sent them a recap of what was going on at the base in Rhode Island where I had been assigned. In fact, I sent an invitation to my boss and other important management people to visit the base when next they were in the general area. They thought this was a great idea. As each one of them came anywhere near Rhode Island, they would let me know in advance. When they came to the base, I would not meet them at the gate. I would have two Marines pick them up in a Jeep and bring them to my office. They would always be suitably impressed with this maneuver. Then I would take them to the beautiful Officer's Club for lunch or dinner. They would be given a tour of the base befitting a high government official. They would then be returned to the gate by the Marines, who would stand by to make sure that the rental car started. As each one of them went back to the home office, he had stories to tell. Some of those stories got back to me. The visibility program was still working. It was impressing the right people.

When my two years were up, I was again released to inactive duty. I reported to my district manager in the Boston area and announced that I was ready to go back to work. I asked if I could have my old territory. He said, "No." I said, "But that was the deal. You said when I left for the service that upon my return I could have my old territory back." He said, "That's right. I did say that. But I won't give you your old territory back. You're going to be a district sales manager. This district. And for your information, they held up my own promotion for three months until you got out." He really wasn't annoyed. I could see from his expression that he was very happy for me. And in turn I was very happy for him. I learned later that the company had not penalized him all that much. For the past six months his salary had been in consonance with the next step up—that of regional sales manager.

I relate this story because it proves a point. Here I had been with the company only one year. In the three-year period that had elapsed I had been on territory one year and in the navy two years. Yet, upon my return, the promotion was waiting. Do I attribute it to my brilliance, my sales expertise, my sales record, my personality? No, none of the above. I attribute this leap into management to nothing more than my visibility program. And I was one of 325. You are most likely one of a group of no more than 12 to 20 field sales managers.

So, I say to you, make yourself visible. As often as you possibly can. I know it will do wonders for you. How do I know? It's simple. Most people are as lazy as they dare to be. While you're doing all this communicating with the home office, the other field sales managers in the organization will be saying to themselves, "I really should write a memo on this." Only, they don't. And as time goes by, the information becomes obsolete, and the memo never gets written. Don't let it happen to you. Do you want to make the future a lot clearer? Make yourself a lot more visible.

Are Your Capabilities Being Recognized?

You've reached the point where you're singing the old tune. The other field sales managers in our organization are not as capable as I am, but they have better territories in bigger metropolitan areas, with higher sales. They're apt to get farther. All because they happen to be at the right place at the right time. It's obvious, you say, from this vantage point that my capabilities simply won't be recognized.

Well, this definitely could be a problem. The field sales manager who's responsible for such large areas as New York, Chicago, Los Angeles, Boston, or Atlanta is always apt to be looked up to. That individual always has more people to supervise, a larger budget, a bigger percentage of national sales. But there are two ways of looking at this. You can accept it as fact and assume that you'll have to get in line for any future promotion, or you can look upon the situation as a challenge, no matter what the odds may be. You know, while the larger metropolitan areas are very glamorous, as well as important to the home office, the degree of turnover in those areas is always greater. The reason for that is quite standard. These areas require more stamina, more expertise, more hours of work, more of everything. The result? Unless the field sales manager is a top-notcher, he or she soon fails.

But I'm not suggesting that you should wait around for someone to fail. That's a ridiculous way to approach anything. In addition to promoting yourself through visibility you can also enhance the rate at which your capabilities will be recognized through flexibility. If you are flexible, in every sense of the word, you'll become a very important commodity.

For example, if you feel that you are not in a large metropolitan area now but would like to be, have you told the home office of this desire? Or if not that specific desire, have you told the proper management officials that you are available for any assignment in the company, whether it be a sales management position in another area or a home office position in a related area?

In many companies a product manager at the home office has greater responsibility and earns more money than a field sales manager. Are you flexible enough to fill one of those positions when and if it became available? The home office would like to know that. Strangely enough, they sometimes assume that you are interested only in the next position in line in the sales field. As openings occur at the home office, they are apt to move up individuals who are already there or to recruit from the outside. There may be an opening in advertising or public relations or market research that you could easily fill. Let's face it, a move to the home office is always a step in the right direction. The question is, do they know about this flexibility?

In addition to flexibility there are other ways in which you can have your capabilities recognized. Your sales meetings are a showcase for you. There is usually someone attending your sales meeting from the home office. That someone, regardless of position in the company, always goes back and reports on what took place. How do you fare at a sales meeting? Have you practiced your public speaking so that you come across well? Do you *read* your speech? If you do, you're not very unusual. Anybody can read a speech. And don't rationalize. Don't hang your hat on the fact that although you may read a speech, you look up a great deal. I've discovered that the more that people look up, the more often they lose their place.

Become a master of the spoken word. When you give a speech at your sales meeting, make sure that it's strictly from the heart, rather than from the paper. And I don't mean that you should memorize it. No way. Before the meeting takes place, develop an outline of your talk. Write it out. Think about it. Collect your thoughts. Then the night before the meeting have the guts to tear it up and throw it away. Then you can approach the podium knowing full well that you are going to deliver a message that comes straight from the heart.

I know exactly what you're thinking. When you speak that way, extemporaneously, you are apt to make mistakes in grammar. You are apt not to use big, important words. So what? People aren't listening to you from the standpoint of how good your grammar is. People never listen to you from the standpoint of how big the words are that you are using. They're listening only because they want to learn something from you. They want a message. They want to take something away with them. And the only way that you can put this across is by speaking right off the cuff.

And speaking of sales meetings, they should always end on the upbeat. No sales meeting should ever come to an end without a strong, enthusiastic, inspirational message. You, as the field sales manager, are the one to deliver it. Always place yourself at the end of the program as well as in other spots. But in closing a meeting you can cover yourself with glory. They always remember what they heard last. They will remember what you said and, more importantly, *how* you said it. As I said, the meeting is a showcase. Even if no one from the home office is present, word will eventually get back. But usually someone will attend, and that someone will be suitably impressed. Do that enough times and your capabilities will never go unnoticed.

One final thought regarding your capabilities. As you well know, for the most part your value is measured by how well you can lead people. Your leadership qualities must always shine. Strangely enough, however, the field sales manager who experiences a high rate of turnover is usually faulted for this. The turnover is usually considered a reflection of the relationship that exists between sales manager and his or her salespeople. Now, this is not necessarily true, but I need not discuss how difficult it is to change the pet ideas of certain people. So, why not make sure that this doesn't happen to you? You can greatly control the amount of turnover by doing three significant things:

- Always do a very thorough job of recruiting and selecting salespeople. Spend as much time as necessary to get the best possible candidates for your openings. (Most field sales managers will hire someone quickly just to fill a territory and regret it sooner or later.)
- Maintain a bullpen. By having several good candidates standing by, whenever a territory becomes available, you will avoid the usual scrambling and the settling for less-qualified people. A bullpen is like an insurance policy.
- Make certain that you have established the type of relationship with every one of your sales representatives that allows them to reach you at any time and discuss with you any problem. Many an individual can be salvaged if there is an opportunity to discuss a given problem before resignation becomes imminent.

If your people know that they can come to you with any type of problem at any time, they will go to the extent of discussing a possible job change with you *before* it is an accomplished fact.

Are You Ready to Give Up?

You have been a field sales manager for a number of years, and many things have happened from time to time that have almost forced you to resign. Maybe a promotion was given to someone else when you thought it was rightfully yours. Maybe you resented something that was said to you by your boss. Whatever the reason, there were probably times when you felt like throwing in the towel. But you didn't. You stuck it out. You felt that at some point your time would come. It was just a case of gaining the proper amount of seniority.

At least that's the way you read it. You second-guessed. You felt reasonably certain that your evaluation of your own situation was well founded.

But here you are, still waiting and nothing has happened. What's the answer? Has the time come to move on? When do you know that it's time? Do you go to the most formidable competitor and make yourself available? Or is this the time to change industries?

This is a tough problem. Perhaps the toughest in this entire book. It's extremely difficult to advise anyone as to what they should do under these circumstances. No two situations are alike. No two companies are alike. There are no true guidelines. There is no record of experience that delineates the specific trend. Just when you think a trend is evolving, something happens that changes everything.

To begin with, you will recall that in the introduction of this book I mentioned the fact that there is a statistic about sales managers that remains constant: Every four years a sales manager changes jobs. This could be by promotion or by dismissal or by resignation. Whatever the case, four years seems to be the length of the average stint. I hasten to add that it's an average. This means that for every sales manager who changes jobs well after four years have elapsed, there is a significant number who didn't last even the four years. It's uncanny, however, to note how closely this four-year statistic seems to hit home.

When it's all said and done, you will have to agree that a four-year period is a long enough span of time to evaluate an individual's leadership qualities in the sales arena, even if far removed from the home office. That individual has gone through forty-eight months of sales management, four budget years, sixteen sales quarters, and anywhere from eight to sixteen or more sales meetings, not including national meetings. This is a long time. It's certainly enough to find out what makes an individual tick. So, if four years have gone by and nothing has happened to you in the way of promotion, and you don't see anything on the horizon, chances are you've been passed over. But wait. **Don't** jump to that conclusion. Even though the reasoning is logical, it isn't necessarily so. Some companies move much more slowly than others. And some companies have a habit of grooming individuals without telling them. So, to assume anything is dangerous.

After four years at the field sales manager level, it would not seem inappropriate for any individual to ask top management what is in store. Why not? You have been training your salespeople to ask for the order over and over again. You have been quite upset when you have made field visits with sales representatives who asked for the order only once or who failed to ask at all. So why can't you ask where you stand? The worst that could happen is that you would find out the truth. And if the truth hurts, so be it. At least you asked and you found out. And you can map out your life accordingly.

Believe it or not, I have consulted with some companies where promotions given to field sales managers were not only based on their capabilities but also based on whether or not they asked for the job. And rightly so. The person who wants to be promoted and says so should never be faulted. It reflects ambition, a willingness to grow, and a definite intent to make a career within the company. At the other end of the spectrum is the individual who never says a word. Never asks about anything. To that person a promotion might still be offered. But what might also happen is that home office management officials will assume that he or she is very happy in the present job and therefore not necessarily eager to move out of the area. When there are small children involved, this is an assumption that comes about more frequently. The only way to erase it is to make known what your intentions are.

I am amused at how many sales managers are impressed by candidates for sales jobs who ask, during the initial interview, "How long do you suppose it will take me to get promoted into management?" And yet these very same sales managers do not turn around and impress management officials by asking the very same question of them about themselves. Now suppose you've been a sales manager for as long as six or even eight years and nothing has happened to you in the way of promotion. Suppose you have asked, every so often, and have been told that you are doing a great job and when the time is right and the opportunity presents itself, you will be well taken care of. The years go by, and nothing happens. What's the answer to that one?

Here again, there is no specific answer, but a few guidelines are in order. If you have been with a growing company for, say, over six years at the field sales manager level and you have seen many opportunities pass you by, and you have probably noted that individuals with much less seniority have been promoted, you most likely have been passed over. It is perhaps time for you to make a change if you are unhappy with your present level of responsibility. If you *are* happy, which means that you like your company, you like your work, and you enjoy each day as much as the previous one, then you should consider making no move whatsoever. This is assuming that you are fully aware of the salary range of your position and that once you have reached its top figure, you're ability to get future raises becomes virtually nonexistent. If you can live with that situation and you *are* happy, what difference does it make? We all know how many people have gone into sales and stayed at that level without ever getting into sales management throughout an entire career. They were happy. They lived a good life. Many of them never saw themselves in sales management and never tried to reach that goal. Not everyone is cut out for management. Not everyone is cut out for top management.

But if your ambitions are such that you feel stymied and want to move on, don't just talk about it, do something about it. But before you go off and accept another job with another company, show a substantial amount of loyalty to your present company. That loyalty, more often than not, is well deserved. Tell the company what you have in mind. You will be amazed at the understanding that you will receive. Especially if the company has no intention of promoting you . They will give you all the assistance possible in order to make the move that you want to make easier for you. It is not unheard of for field sales managers to be given as much as three months to resituate themselves and yet stay on the payroll. I've seen field sales managers be allowed to keep their company cars for as long as six months until they found the right situation and obtained a company car from their new association. The amount of consideration that is generally shown by most companies in this country defies description. So, under those circumstances, why wouldn't you be loyal? Why wouldn't you lay your cards on the table and have a frank discussion with your superior? Certainly you always expected this from your sales representatives. Why not turn around and offer it in the other direction?

But I will not, under any circumstances, end this book on a negative note. Even though there are all kinds of ways of solving problems, including the ones just described, there are also ways of avoiding them. So, why not avoid reaching this point to begin with? Most salespeople defeat themselves. If they don't make it in sales, it's because they didn't try hard enough. It's no different with sales managers. They defeat themselves more often than not.

You need not let this happen to you. Make sure that you follow as many suggestions as are available to you as early in the game as possible. Put everything you have into your job. Maintain a positive mental attitude at all times. And keep an open mind about any and all things that might help you to be more successful. There is a wealth of information available to those who are interested. This book is only one of many. Read as much as you can about your job. And then apply it wherever possible.

When it's all said and done, you can always take great pride in knowing that your job is a very important one. You have every reason to hold your head up high. The field sales manager is much like the sergeant in the army. Top brass makes a lot of decisions, but they're quite worthless if the sergeant out in the field doesn't see that his men carry them out.

So many times we have heard the question, "Where would our economy be if the members of the selling profession weren't out there every day making the wheels turn?" Well, much the same could be said for people like you. Where would our economy be if the field sales managers weren't out there to make sure that those who sell put in a decent day's work—every single day?

Index